Penguin's Poems
for Weddings

Laura Barber is a former editorial director for Penguin Classics and now publishes contemporary literature and writes. She also selected and introduced *Penguin's Poems for Life*, *Penguin's Poems for Love* and *Penguin's Poems by Heart*.

Penguin's Poems
for Weddings

Selected with a preface by
LAURA BARBER

PENGUIN CLASSICS
an imprint of
PENGUIN BOOKS

PENGUIN CLASSICS

Published by the Penguin Group
Penguin Books Ltd, 80 Strand, London WC2R ORL, England
Penguin Group (USA) Inc., 375 Hudson Street, New York, New York 10014, USA
Penguin Group (Canada), 90 Eglinton Avenue East, Suite 700, Toronto, Ontario, Canada M4P 2Y3
(a division of Pearson Penguin Canada Inc.)
Penguin Ireland, 25 St Stephen's Green, Dublin 2, Ireland (a division of Penguin Books Ltd)
Penguin Group (Australia), 707 Collins Street, Melbourne, Victoria 3008, Australia
(a division of Pearson Australia Group Pty Ltd)
Penguin Books India Pvt Ltd, 11 Community Centre, Panchsheel Park, New Delhi – 110 017, India
Penguin Group (NZ), 67 Apollo Drive, Rosedale, Auckland 0632, New Zealand
(a division of Pearson New Zealand Ltd)
Penguin Books (South Africa) (Pty) Ltd, Block D, Rosebank Office Park,
181 Jan Smuts Avenue, Parktown North, Gauteng 2193, South Africa

Penguin Books Ltd, Registered Offices: 80 Strand, London WC2R ORL, England

www.penguin.com

This selection first published in Penguin Classics 2014
001

Selection and editorial material copyright © Laura Barber, 2014

Cover design Coralie Bickford-Smith

The moral right of the editor has been asserted

The Acknowledgements on pages 193–197 constitute an extension of this copyright page

Set in 11/13.5pt Adobe Sabon
Typeset by Jouve (UK), Milton Keynes
Printed in Great Britain by Clays Ltd, St Ives plc

A CIP catalogue record for this book is available from the British Library

ISBN: 978-0-141-39469-5

www.greenpenguin.co.uk

Contents

Declarations

Promises

Celebrations

Continuations

Out of your whole life give but a moment!
All of your life that has gone before,
All to come after it, – so you ignore,
So you make perfect the present, – condense,
In a rapture of rage, for perfection's endowment,
Thought and feeling and soul and sense –
Merged in a moment which gives me at last
You around me for once, you beneath me, above me –
Me – sure that despite of time future, time past, –
This tick of our life-time's one moment you love me!
How long such suspension may linger? Ah, Sweet,
The moment's eternal – just that and no more –
When ecstasy's utmost we clutch at the core
While cheeks burn, arms open, eyes shut and lips meet!

Robert Browning,
Now

Preface

In the lifetime of a couple's love, a wedding is but a moment. But it is a big moment and one that seems to defy the normal laws of time and space – for it contains within it not only the present but an entire imagined future. Supercharged with emotion and expectation, the moment of a wedding is like a starburst that dazzles in the instant and shines out bright in the memory, bright enough – one trusts – to illuminate the days of darkness or challenge that might come. In such a moment, as hopes blaze towards eternity, every word counts: not just the 'I' and the 'do', but all the other words that cluster around them. And so, we might find something reassuring and right in the repetition of those formal, time-buffed phrases that sit at the heart of a traditional religious ceremony: 'I take you', 'to love and to cherish', 'from this day forward', 'I thee wed'. Or we might compose our own vows, handwritten lines that resonate with personal significance. And we might also turn to poetry – where language is compressed into its most potent, brilliant form. At this moment a poem can encapsulate feelings in words, pin them down, seal them up for future reference. It can become, like love itself, an 'ever-fixèd mark', as Shakespeare puts it, 'the star to every wandering bark', as two people navigate the uncharted seas of life together.

Finding the perfect wedding poem can be a daunting prospect – especially if you're not a lifelong poetry-lover, just someone who wants a poem to mark the occasion. So that's where this book comes in. Here you will find a wide range of poems, from the classic to the contemporary, and from the deeply romantic to the resolutely realistic. Of course, trying to make a choice from even a shortlist of several centuries' worth of love poetry is just as tricky as whittling down a guest list, and indeed, I've found arranging the poems here about as fraught as settling on a seating plan, not least because I wanted them to be able to mingle. But, as I read the poems aloud, I tried to listen closely to what they were actually saying and gradually they began to form natural groupings.

We begin, then, with 'Proposals': one person inviting another to envisage a shared future. These are poems with an edge of vulnerability: they beseech; they urge; they whisper sweet somethings; they hold out a hand; they attempt to nonchalantly indicate that, were the other person so inclined, they, too, wouldn't be entirely averse to making a go of it. These are poems that yearn for an answer. In 'Declarations' the mood moves from contingency to confidence: many of these poems are buoyed, almost to giddiness, by the knowledge that this love is real and reciprocated; others are anchored by a certainty that this bond will last. The poems in 'Promises' go further and swear, on this present love, to keep faith 'for ever', 'for always', 'unto death', 'till the world were done', till 'the rocks melt wi' the sun'. A relationship (ideally) contains only two people, but a wedding (legally) demands at least five, so 'Celebrations' is a more public affair, shifting the focus from deeply personal expressions of devotion to poems that reflect on love from the outside. These are poems that are easy for a third person to read without feeling like a gooseberry or a peeping Tom. And because the day itself is only the beginning of commitment, the final section is dedicated to what happens after the last drop of champagne has been drunk and the honeyed moon has slipped beyond the horizon, during the long stretch of time in which the strength of those pledges is put to the test. These are the poems that take a true measure of love, making accommodations for the ebbs and flows of passion, and the storms and tempests of domestic discord, to reset bearings and love on. Gathered at the end of the book is the 'Confetti', snippets of verse intended for scattering as you like, on invitations, in an order of service, as place-settings or in wedding favours.

Though the poems in these sections are speaking to roughly similar stages in a relationship, their form of expression varies widely, from folk ballad to nursery rhyme, via sonnet, song lyric, litany and free verse. And their voices, drawn from various corners of the English-speaking world, are very different too: some serious, some mischievous, some reaching the heights of rhapsody, some steadily plain-spoken. But whether you are looking for something that adds a touch of gravitas or brings a dash of levity, I hope you will be able to find at least one poem that chimes with the tone of your wedding.

And, of course, a wedding today is a much, altered thing from what it was when Chaucer's Franklin described the harmony between a chivalrous knight and his humble lady or when Milton retold the story of Adam and Eve, and even from when Elizabeth Barrett and Robert Browning conducted their secret courtship and plotted to elope. Today a wedding might occur at any point in a relationship; it might be gay or straight; it might take place barefoot in a meadow, before a registry desk, beneath a canopy or a vaulted ceiling; it might be a casual gathering of friends and an excuse for a party or it might involve standing side by side in front of a vast congregation. What hasn't changed, though, over all these centuries, is the impulse that many people feel for some kind of rite to mark their love – what Peter Meinke's poem 'The First Marriage' describes as an 'inchoate / need for ceremony a desire for witness'. Poets understand this need and they meet it, with ritual words that have been polished until they sparkle. It is no accident, I think, that so many poems about love look skyward and glimpse there a vast galaxy by which the course of love might be plotted, from Langston Hughes's starlit stroll in Manhattan to Anne MacLeod's unending dance beneath the 'wheeling, circling stars' of Cuillin; from Keats's steadfast 'bright star' to Edith Wharton's 'setting star'; and from Billy Collins's 'shooting star' to R. S. Thomas's 'luminary' lover; and back again to Shakespeare's unshakable celestial 'mark'. A poem, like a wedding, captures but a moment in love, but it can help to make that moment glow for ever.

A Note on the Poems

All the poems included here were written in English, with the exception of the excerpts from the Bible. Beyond this, my aim has been to range as widely as possible, historically and geographically. The earliest poem in the selection was composed in the fourteenth century and the most recent are only just appearing in print. The poets themselves come from all parts of the world, including Iran, India, South America, the Bahamas, the United States of America and Canada, Australia, the United Kingdom and the Republic of Ireland.

For ease of comprehension – and reading aloud – punctuation and spelling in the older poems have been lightly modernized, and glosses have been provided for the dialect poems of Robert Burns. Where a definitive text has been established by editors (for example, Emily Dickinson) and for all modern works, the poems are reproduced exactly as published.

Proposals

LANGSTON HUGHES

Harlem Night Song

Come,
Let us roam the night together
Singing.

I love you.

Across
The Harlem roof-tops
Moon is shining.
Night sky is blue.
Stars are great drops
Of golden dew.

Down the street
A band is playing.

I love you.

Come,
Let us roam the night together
Singing.

ANONYMOUS

Madam, Will You Walk?

'I should like to buy thee a fine lace cap
With five yards of ribbon to hang down your back
If thou wilt walk with me.'

'I will not accept of the fine lace cap
With the five yards of ribbon to hang down my back
Nor I will not walk with thee.'

'I will buy thee a fine silken gown
With nine yards of ribbon to trail upon the ground
If thou wilt walk with me.'

'I will not accept of the fine silken gown
With nine yards of ribbon to trail upon the ground
Nor I won't walk with thee.'

'I'll buy thee a fine golden chair
To sit in the garden and to take the pleasant air
If thou wilt walk with me.'

'I will not accept of thy fine golden chair
To sit in the garden and to take the pleasant air
Nor I will not walk with thee.'

'It's I will give thee the keys of my chest
To take gold and silver when thou art distressed
If thou wilt walk with me.'

'I will not accept of the keys of your chest
To take gold and silver when I am distressed
Nor I will not walk with thee.'

'I'll give thee the key, O the key of my heart
And thy heart and my heart shall never depart
If thou wilt walk with me.'

'I will accept of the key of your heart
And thy heart and my heart shall never depart
And I will walk with thee.'

LEWIS CARROLL

The Mock Turtle's Song

from *Alice's Adventures in Wonderland*

'Will you walk a little faster?' said a whiting to a snail,
'There's a porpoise close behind us, and he's treading on my tail.
See how eagerly the lobsters and the turtles all advance!
They are waiting on the shingle – will you come and join the
     dance?
     Will you, won't you, will you, won't you, will you join
      the dance?
     Will you, won't you, will you, won't you, won't you join
      the dance?

'You can really have no notion how delightful it would be
When they take us up and throw us, with the lobsters, out
     to sea!'
But the snail replied 'Too far, too far!' and gave a look askance –
Said he thanked the whiting kindly, but he would not join the
     dance.
     Would not, could not, would not, could not, would not
      join the dance.
     Would not, could not, would not, could not, could not
      join the dance.

'What matters it how far we go?' his scaly friend replied.
'There is another shore, you know, upon the other side.
The further off from England the nearer is to France –
Then turn not pale, beloved snail, but come and join the dance.
     Will you, won't you, will you, won't you, will you join
      the dance?
     Will you, won't you, will you, won't you, won't you join
      the dance?'

EDMUND SPENSER

from *Amoretti*

LXV

The doubt which ye misdeem, fair Love, is vain,
   That fondly fear to lose your liberty,
   when losing one, two liberties ye gain,
   and make him bound, that bondage erst did fly.
Sweet be the bands, the which true love doth tie,
   without constraint, or dread of any ill:
   the gentle bird feels no captivity
   within her cage, but sings and feeds her fill.
There pride dare not approach, nor discord spill
   the league twixt them, that loyal love hath bound:
   but simple truth and mutual good will,
   seeks with sweet peace to salve each other's wound:
There faith doth fearless dwell in brazen tower,
   and spotless pleasure builds her sacred bower.

JOHN COOPER CLARKE

i wanna be yours

let me be your vacuum cleaner
breathing in your dust
let me be your ford cortina
i will never rust
if you like your coffee hot
let me be your coffee pot
you call the shots
i wanna be yours

let me be your raincoat
for those frequent rainy days
let me be your dreamboat
when you wanna sail away
let me be your teddy bear
take me with you anywhere
i don't care
i wanna be yours

let me be your electric meter
i will not run out
let me be the electric heater
you get cold without
let me be your setting lotion
hold your hair
with deep devotion
deep as the deep
atlantic ocean
that's how deep is my emotion
deep deep deep deep de deep deep
i don't wanna be hers
i wanna be yours

JOHN GAY

from *The Beggar's Opera*

Were I laid on Greenland's coast,
  And in my arms embraced my lass;
Warm amidst eternal frost,
Too soon the half year's night would pass.
Were I sold on Indian soil,
  Soon as the burning day was closed,
I could mock the sultry toil
  When on my charmer's breast reposed.
And I would love you all the day,
Every night would kiss and play,
If with me you'd fondly stray
Over the hills and far away.

ALFRED, LORD TENNYSON

from *The Princess*

Now sleeps the crimson petal, now the white;
Nor waves the cypress in the palace walk;
Nor winks the gold fin in the porphyry font.
The firefly wakens: waken thou with me.

Now droops the milkwhite peacock like a ghost,
And like a ghost she glimmers on to me.

Now lies the Earth all Danaë to the stars,
And all thy heart lies open unto me.

Now slides the silent meteor on, and leaves
A shining furrow, as thy thoughts in me.

Now folds the lily all her sweetness up,
And slips into the bosom of the lake:
So fold thyself, my dearest, thou, and slip
Into my bosom and be lost in me.

ROBERT BURNS

Oh wert thou in the cauld blast,
  On yonder lea, on yonder lea;
My plaidie to the angry airt,
  I'd shelter thee, I'd shelter thee:
Or did misfortune's bitter storms
  Around thee blaw, around thee blaw,
Thy bield should be my bosom,
  To share it a', to share it a'.

Or were I in the wildest waste,
  Sae black and bare, sae black and bare,
The desert were a paradise,
  If thou wert there, if thou wert there.
Or were I monarch o' the globe,
  Wi' thee to reign, wi' thee to reign;
The brightest jewel in my crown,
  Wad be my queen, wad be my queen.

plaidie plaid; *bield* shelter

ANONYMOUS

'Lavender's blue, dilly, dilly, lavender's green,
When I am king, dilly, dilly, you shall be queen.'
'Who told you so, dilly, dilly, who told you so?'
''Twas my own heart, dilly, dilly, that told me so.'

'Call up your men, dilly, dilly, set them to work
Some to the plough, dilly, dilly, some to the fork,
Some to make hay, dilly, dilly, some to cut corn,
While you and I, dilly, dilly, keep ourselves warm.'

'Lavender's green, dilly, dilly, lavender's blue,
If you love me, dilly, dilly, I will love you.
Let the birds sing, dilly, dilly, and the lambs play;
We shall be safe, dilly, dilly, out of harm's way.'

'If it should hap, dilly, dilly, if it should chance,
We shall be gay, dilly, dilly, we shall both dance
Lavender's blue, dilly, dilly, lavender's green,
When you are king, dilly, dilly, I'll be your queen.'

DON PATERSON

The Trans-Siberian Express

(for Eva)

One day we will make our perfect journey –
the great train smashing through Dundee, Brooklyn
and off into the endless tundra,
the earth flattening out before us.

I follow your continuous arrival,
shedding veil after veil after veil –
the automatic doors wincing away
while you stagger back from the buffet

slopping *Laphroaig* and decent coffee
until you face me from that long enfilade
of glass, stretched to vanishing point
like facing mirrors, a lifetime of days.

MICHAEL DONAGHY

The Present

For the present there is just one moon,
though every level pond gives back another.

But the bright disc shining in the black lagoon,
perceived by astrophysicist and lover,

is milliseconds old. And even that light's
seven minutes older than its source.

And the stars we think we see on moonless nights
are long extinguished. And, of course,

this very moment, as you read this line,
is literally gone before you know it.

Forget the here-and-now. We have no time
but this device of wantonness and wit.

Make me this present then: your hand in mine,
and we'll live out our lives in it.

ELIZABETH BARRETT BROWNING

from *Sonnets from the Portuguese*

XXII

When our two souls stand up erect and strong,
Face to face, silent, drawing nigh and nigher,
Until the lengthening wings break into fire
At either curvèd point, – what bitter wrong,
Can the earth do to us, that we should not long
Be here contented? – Think. In mounting higher,
The angels would press on us, and aspire
To drop some golden orb of perfect song
Into our deep, dear silence. Let us stay
Rather on earth, beloved, – where the unfit
Contrarious moods of men recoil away
And isolate pure spirits, and permit
A place to stand and love in, for a day,
With darkness and the death-hour rounding it.

If I were loved, as I desire to be,
What is there in the great sphere of the earth,
And range of evil between death and birth,
That I should fear, – if I were loved by thee?
All the inner, all the outer world of pain
Clear love would pierce and cleave, if thou wert mine,
As I have heard that, somewhere in the main,
Fresh-water springs come up through bitter brine.
'Twere joy, not fear, clasped hand-in-hand with thee,
To wait for death – mute – careless of all ills,
Apart upon a mountain, though the surge
Of some new deluge from a thousand hills
Flung leagues of roaring foam into the gorge
Below us, as far on as eye could see.

JOHN FLETCHER

O divine star of Heaven,
Thou in power above the seven;
Thou sweet kindler of desires
Till they grow to mutual fires;
Thou, O gentle Queen, that art
Curer of each wounded heart;
Thou the fuel, and the flame;
Thou in heaven, and here, the same;
Thou the wooer, and the wooed;
Thou the hunger, and the food;
Thou the prayer, and the prayed;
Thou what is or shall be said.
Thou still young, and golden tressed,
Make me by thy answer blessed.

THE KING JAMES BIBLE

from *The Song of Solomon*

Come with me from Lebanon, my spouse, with me from Lebanon: look from the top of Amana, from the top of Shenir, and Hermon, from the lions' dens, from the mountains of the leopards.

Thou hast ravished my heart, my sister, my spouse; thou hast ravished my heart with one of thine eyes, with one chain of thy neck.

How fair is thy love, my sister, my spouse! how much better is thy love than wine! and the smell of thy ointments than all spices!

Thy lips, O my spouse, drop as the honeycomb: honey and milk are under thy tongue; and the smell of thine garments is like the smell of Lebanon.

A garden enclosed is my sister, my spouse; a spring shut up, a fountain sealed.

Thy plants are an orchard of pomegranates, with pleasant fruits; camphire, with spikenard,

Spikenard and saffron; calamus and cinnamon, with all trees of frankincense; myrrh and aloes, with all the chief spices.

A fountain of gardens, a well of living waters, and streams from Lebanon.

Awake, O north wind; and come, thou south; blow upon my garden, that the spices thereof may flow out. Let my beloved come into his garden, and eat his pleasant fruits.

THOMAS HOOD

Ruth

She stood breast-high amid the corn,
Clasped by the golden light of morn,
Like the sweetheart of the sun,
Who many a glowing kiss had won.

On her cheek an autumn flush,
Deeply ripened; – such a blush
In the midst of brown was born,
Like red poppies grown with corn.

Round her eyes her tresses fell,
Which were blackest none could tell,
But long lashes veiled a light,
That had else been all too bright.

And her hat, with shady brim,
Made her tressy forehead dim; –
Thus she stood amid the stooks,
Praising God with sweetest looks: –

Sure, I said, heaven did not mean,
Where I reap thou shouldst but glean,
Lay thy sheaf adown and come,
Share my harvest and my home.

ANONYMOUS

Sukey, you shall be my wife
And I will tell you why:
I have got a little pig,
And you have got a sty;
I have got a dun cow,
And you can make good cheese.
Sukey, will you marry me?
Say Yes, if you please.

GEORGE HERBERT

Love

Love bade me welcome: yet my soul drew back,
      Guilty of dust and sin.
But quick-eyed Love, observing me grow slack
      From my first entrance in,
Drew nearer to me, sweetly questioning,
      If I lacked any thing.

A guest, I answered, worthy to be here:
      Love said, You shall be he.
I the unkind, ungrateful? Ah my dear,
      I cannot look on thee.
Love took my hand, and smiling did reply,
      Who made the eyes but I?

Truth, Lord, but I have marred them: let my shame
      Go where it doth deserve.
And know you not, says Love, who bore the blame?
      My dear, then I will serve.
You must sit down, says Love, and taste my meat:
      So I did sit and eat.

IAN GREGORY STRACHAN

i must share these with you

here, then, is the crux of it

this wave of guava
that embraces me in the backyard
this melody of sugar cane
that makes me shut my eyes
this mellow coolness
of the avocado on my tongue
this terrible delight
of salt water about my shoulders

here is the crux of it

the joy i feel atop this hill
watching the sea tickle reef
this giddiness that comes
with the coconut water spilling
this sloppy pleasure i take
in the sugar apple
this fearless gallop
on the crab grass, laughing

here, black woman, is the crux of it:
i must share these with you

WALT WHITMAN

from *Song of the Open Road*

Listen! I will be honest with you,
I do not offer the old smooth prizes, but offer
  rough new prizes,
These are the days that must happen to you:
You shall not heap up what is called riches,
You shall scatter with lavish hand all that you
  earn or achieve [. . .]

Camerado, I give you my hand!
I give you my love more precious than money,
I give you myself before preaching or law;
Will you give me yourself? will you come travel
  with me?
Shall we stick by each other as long as we live?

CHRISTOPHER MARLOWE

The Passionate Shepherd to His Love

Come live with me, and be my love,
And we will all the pleasures prove
That valleys, groves, hills and fields,
Woods or steepy mountains yield.

And will we sit upon the rocks,
Seeing the shepherds feed their flocks
By shallow rivers, to whose falls
Melodious birds sing madrigals.

And I will make thee beds of roses,
And a thousand fragrant posies,
A cap of flowers, and a kirtle
Embroidered all with leaves of myrtle.

A gown made of the finest wool
Which from our pretty lambs we pull,
Fair linèd slippers for the cold,
With buckles of the purest gold.

A belt of straw, and ivy buds,
With coral clasps and amber studs,
And if these pleasures may thee move,
Come live with me, and be my love.

The shepherd swains shall dance and sing
For thy delight each May morning.
If these delights thy mind may move;
Then live with me and be my love.

ELIZABETH BARRETT BROWNING

from *Sonnets from the Portuguese*

XIV

If thou must love me, let it be for nought
Except for love's sake only. Do not say
'I love her for her smile – her look – her way
Of speaking gently, – for a trick of thought
That falls in well with mine, and certes brought
A sense of pleasant ease on such a day –'
For these things in themselves, beloved, may
Be changed, or change for thee, – and love so wrought,
May be unwrought so. Neither love me for
Thine own dear pity wiping my cheeks dry –
For one might well forget to weep, who bore
Thy comfort long, and lose thy love thereby –
But love me for love's sake, that evermore
Thou may'st love on, through love's eternity.

NICK LAIRD

Estimates

Who knows what you mean by love?
Extrapolating from the facts
you want two hundred friends
to watch
you wear the white and walk the aisle.

We could pack the car and motor north
to waterfall and rock, a nightfall
lit by moonlight on the snowfall
patches
still intact among the sheep-tracks

and the turf-banks and the heather.
We could pull in somewhere there,
kill the engine, wait,
listen
to a late-night country music station,

split bars of dark and fruit-&-nut,
sip amaretto from the lid, skin up,
and wake,
unwashed and cramped
as man and wife

in a place unpeopled, dawn-calm,
cleared of its gestures, its features
by weather, to mountains,
and mountains of clouds.
We could.

WILLIAM MEREDITH

Tree Marriage

In Chota Nagpur and Bengal
the betrothed are tied with threads to
mango trees, they marry the trees
as well as one another, and
the two trees marry each other.
Could we do that some time with oaks
or beeches? This gossamer we
hold each other with, this web
of love and habit is not enough.
In mistrust of heavier ties,
I would like tree-siblings for us,
standing together somewhere, two
trees married with us, lightly, their
fingers barely touching in sleep,
our threads invisible but holding.

JOHN KEATS

This living hand, now warm and capable
Of earnest grasping, would, if it were cold
And in the icy silence of the tomb,
So haunt thy days and chill thy dreaming nights
That thou would wish thine own heart dry of blood
So in my veins red life might stream again,
And thou be conscience-calmed – see here it is –
I hold it towards you.

It was a quiet way –
He asked if I was his –
I made no answer of the Tongue
But answer of the Eyes –
And then He bore me on
Before this mortal noise
With swiftness, as of Chariots
And distance, as of Wheels.
This World did drop away
As Acres from the feet
Of one that leaneth from Balloon
Upon an Ether street.
The Gulf behind was not,
The Continents were new –
Eternity it was before
Eternity was due.
No Seasons were to us –
It was not Night nor Morn –
But Sunrise stopped upon the place
And fastened it in Dawn.

Declarations

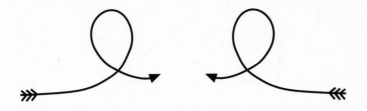

FRANK O'HARA

Poem

Light   clarity   avocado salad in the morning
after all the terrible things I do how amazing it is
to find forgiveness and love, not even forgiveness
since what is done is done and forgiveness isn't love
and love is love nothing can ever go wrong
though things can get irritating boring and dispensable
(in the imagination) but not really for love
though a block away you feel distant the mere presence
changes everything like a chemical dropped on a paper
and all thoughts disappear in a strange quiet excitement
I am sure of nothing but this, intensified by breathing

JOHN DONNE

The Good-Morrow

I wonder, by my troth, what thou and I
Did, till we loved? Were we not weaned till then?
But sucked on country pleasures, childishly?
Or snorted we in the seven sleepers' den?
'Twas so; but this, all pleasures fancies be.
If ever any beauty I did see,
Which I desired, and got, 'twas but a dream of thee.

And now good morrow to our waking souls,
Which watch not one another out of fear;
For love, all love of other sights controls,
And makes one little room, an everywhere.
Let sea-discoverers to new worlds have gone,
Let maps to others, worlds on worlds have shown,
Let us possess one world, each hath one, and is one.

My face in thine eye, thine in mine appears,
And true plain hearts do in the faces rest;
Where can we find two better hemispheres,
Without sharp North, without declining West?
Whatever dies, was not mixed equally;
If our two loves be one, or, thou and I
Love so alike, that none do slacken, none can die.

ANNE BRADSTREET

To My Dear and Loving Husband

If ever two were one, then surely we.
If ever man were loved by wife, then thee.
If ever wife was happy in a man,
Compare with me, ye women, if you can.
I prize thy love more than whole mines of gold,
Or all the riches that the East doth hold.
My love is such that rivers cannot quench,
Nor aught but love from thee give recompense.
Thy love is such I can no way repay,
The heavens reward thee manifold, I pray.
Then while we live, in love let's so perséver,
That when we live no more, we may live ever.

MICHAEL DRAYTON

Verses Made the Night Before He Died

So well I love thee, as without thee I
Love nothing; if I might choose, I'd rather die
Than be one day debarred thy company.

Since beasts, and plants do grow, and live and move,
Beasts are those men, that such a life approve:
He only lives, that deadly is in love.

The corn that in the ground is sown first dies
And of one seed do many ears arise:
Love, this world's corn, by dying multiplies.

The seeds of love first by thy eyes were thrown
Into a ground untilled, a heart unknown
To bear such fruit, till by thy hands 'twas sown.

Look as thy looking glass by chance may fall,
Divide and break in many pieces small
And yet shows forth the selfsame face in all:

Proportions, features, graces just the same,
And in the smallest piece as well the name
Of fairest one deserves, as in the richest frame.

So all my thoughts are pieces but of you
Which put together makes a glass so true
As I therein no other's face but yours can view.

EDWIN MUIR

The Confirmation

Yes, yours, my love, is the right human face.
I in my mind had waited for this long,
Seeing the false and searching for the true,
Then found you as a traveller finds a place
Of welcome suddenly amid the wrong
Valleys and rocks and twisting roads. But you,
What shall I call you? A fountain in a waste,
A well of water in a country dry,
Or anything that's honest and good, an eye
That makes the whole world bright. Your open heart,
Simple with giving, gives the primal deed,
The first good world, the blossom, the blowing seed,
The hearth, the steadfast land, the wandering sea,
Not beautiful or rare in every part,
But like yourself, as they were meant to be.

WILLIAM BARNES

With you first shown to me,
With you first known to me,
My life-time loom'd, in hope, a length of joy:
Your voice so sweetly spoke,
Your mind so meetly spoke,
My hopes were all of bliss without alloy,
As I, for your abode, sought out, with pride,
This house with vines o'er-ranging all its side.

I thought of years to come,
All free of tears to come,
When I might call you mine, and mine alone,
With steps to fall for me,
And day cares all for me,
And hands for ever nigh to help my own;
And then thank'd Him who had not cast my time
Too early or too late for your sweet prime.

Then day was dawn, o'er dew,
And day withdrawn, o'er dew,
And mid-day glow'd on flow'rs along the ledge,
And walls in sight, afar,
Were shining white, afar,
And brightly shone the stream behind the sedge.
But still, the fairest light of those clear days
Seem'd that which fell along your flow'ry ways.

KAMALA DAS

Love

Until I found you,
I wrote verse, drew pictures,
And, went out with friends
For walks . . .
Now that I love you,
Curled like an old mongrel
My life lies, content,
In you . . .

BILLY COLLINS

Litany

You are the bread and the knife,
The crystal goblet and the wine.

Jacques Crickillon

You are the bread and the knife,
the crystal goblet and the wine.
You are the dew on the morning grass,
and the burning wheel of the sun.
You are the white apron of the baker
and the marsh birds suddenly in flight.

However, you are not the wind in the orchard,
the plums on the counter,
or the house of cards.
And you are certainly not the pine-scented air.
There is no way you are the pine-scented air.

It is possible that you are the fish under the bridge,
maybe even the pigeon on the general's head,
but you are not even close
to being the field of cornflowers at dusk.

And a quick look in the mirror will show
that you are neither the boots in the corner
nor the boat asleep in its boathouse.

It might interest you to know,
speaking of the plentiful imagery of the world,
that I am the sound of rain on the roof.

I also happen to be the shooting star,
the evening paper blowing down an alley,
and the basket of chestnuts on the kitchen table.

I am also the moon in the trees
and the blind woman's teacup.
But don't worry, I am not the bread and the knife.
You are still the bread and the knife.
You will always be the bread and the knife,
not to mention the crystal goblet and – somehow – the wine.

ALICE OSWALD

Wedding

From time to time our love is like a sail
and when the sail begins to alternate
from tack to tack, it's like a swallowtail
and when the swallow flies it's like a coat;
and if the coat is yours, it has a tear
like a wide mouth and when the mouth begins
to draw the wind, it's like a trumpeter
and when the trumpet blows, it blows like millions . . .
and this, my love, when millions come and go
beyond the need of us, is like a trick;
and when the trick begins, it's like a toe
tip-toeing on a rope, which is like luck;
and when the luck begins, it's like a wedding,
which is like love, which is like everything.

SIR PHILIP SIDNEY

from *The Countess of Pembroke's Arcadia*

My true love hath my heart, and I have his,
By just exchange one for the other given:
I hold his dear, and mine he cannot miss;
There never was a better bargain driven.
His heart in me keeps me and him in one,
My heart in him his thoughts and senses guides:
He loves my heart, for once it was his own;
I cherish his because in me it bides.
His heart his wound received from my sight;
My heart was wounded with his wounded heart;
For as from me, on him his hurt did light,
So still methought in me his hurt did smart.
   Both equal hurt, in this change sought our bliss:
   My true love hath my heart, and I have his.

SIR JOHN SUCKLING

The Stolen Heart

I prithee send me back my heart,
Since I cannot have thine;
For if from yours you will not part,
Why then shouldst thou have mine?

Yet now I think on't, let it lie,
To find it were in vain;
For thou hast a thief in either eye
Would steal it back again.

Why should two hearts in one breast lie,
And yet not lodge together?
O Love! where is thy sympathy,
If thus our breasts thou sever?

But love is such a mystery,
I cannot find it out;
For when I think I'm best resolved,
I then am in most doubt.

Then farewell care, and farewell woe;
I will no longer pine;
For I'll believe I have her heart,
As much as she hath mine.

SOPHIE HANNAH

Match

Love has not made us good.
We still do all the cynics said we would –
Struggle like heroes searching for a war,
Still want too much, and more.

Love has not made us nice.
Elders and betters with their best advice
Can't stir us from the loungers by the pool.
We dodge all work like school,

Leave urgent debts unpaid.
Cancel the solemn promises we've made
If loyalties or circumstances change.
Our thoughts are no less strange,

But love has made us last.
We do together all that in the past
We did alone; err not as one but two
And this is how I knew.

A. S. J. TESSIMOND

Not love perhaps

This is not Love, perhaps – Love that lays down
Its life, that many waters cannot quench, nor the
    floods drown –
But something written in lighter ink, said in a lower tone:
Something, perhaps, especially our own:
A need at times to be together and talk –
And then the finding we can walk
More firmly through dark narrow places
And meet more easily nightmare faces:
A need to reach out sometimes hand to hand –
And then find Earth less like an alien land:
A need for alliance to defeat
The whisperers at the corner of the street:
A need for inns on roads, islands in seas, halts for
    discoveries to be shared,
Maps checked, notes compared:
A need at times of each for each,
Direct as the need of throat and tongue for speech.

from *Paradise Lost,* Book IV

With thee conversing I forget all time,
All seasons and their change, all please alike.
Sweet is the breath of morn, her rising sweet,
With charm of earliest birds; pleasant the sun
When first on this delightful land he spreads
His orient beams, on herb, tree, fruit and flower,
Glistering with dew; fragrant the fertile earth
After soft showers; and sweet the coming on
Of grateful evening mild, then silent night
With this her solemn bird and this fair moon,
And these the gems of heaven, her starry train:
But neither breath of morn when she ascends
With charm of earliest birds, nor rising sun
On this delightful land, nor herb, fruit, flower,
Glistering with dew, nor fragrance after showers,
Nor grateful evening mild, nor silent night
With this her solemn bird, nor walk by moon,
Or glittering starlight without thee is sweet.

CAROL ANN DUFFY

Swing

Someone had looped a rope over a branch
and made a rough swing for the birch tree
next to the river. We passed it, walking and walking
into our new love; soft, unbearable dawns of desire
where mist was the water's slipping veil, or foam
boasted and frothed like champagne at the river's bend.

You asked me if I was sure, as a line of Canada geese
crowded the other bank, happy as wedding guests. Yes,
sure as the vision that flares in my head, away from you now,
of the moment you climbed on the swing, and swung out
into the silver air, the endless affirmative blue,
like something from heaven on earth, from paradise.

FRANCIS QUARLES

Canticle

Even like two little bank-dividing brooks,
    That wash the pebbles with their wanton streams,
And having ranged and searched a thousand nooks,
    Meet both at length in silver-breasted Thames;
        Where, in a greater current they conjoin:
So I my Best-Beloved's am; so he is mine.

Even so we met; and after long pursuit,
    Even so we joined; we both became entire;
No need for either to renew a suit,
    For I was flax and he was flames of fire:
        Our firm united souls did more than twine;
So I my Best-Beloved's am; so he is mine.

If all those glittering monarchs that command
    The servile quarters of this earthly ball
Should tender, in exchange, their shares of land,
    I would not change my fortunes for them all:
        Their wealth is but a counter to my coin;
The world's but theirs, but my Beloved's mine.

Nay, more: if the fair Thespian ladies all
    Should heap together their diviner treasure,
That treasure should be deemed a price too small
    To buy a minute's lease of half my pleasure.
        'Tis not the sacred wealth of all the Nine
Can buy my heart from him; or his, from being mine.

Nor time, nor place, nor chance, nor death can bow
    My least desires unto the least remove;
He's firmly mine by oath; I, his, by vow;
    He's mine by faith; and I am his, by love;
        He's mine by water; I am his, by wine;
Thus I my Best-Beloved's am; thus he is mine.

He is my altar; I, his holy place;
    I am his guest; and he, my living food;
I'm his, by penitence; he, mine by grace;
    I'm his, by purchase; he is mine, by blood;
        He's my supporting elm; and I, his vine:
Thus I my Best-Beloved's am; thus he is mine.

He gives me wealth: I give him all my vows:
    I give him songs; he gives me length of days;
With wreaths of grace he crowns my conquering brows:
    And I, his temples, with a crown of praise,
        Which he accepts as an everlasting sign,
That I my Best-Beloved's am; that he is mine.

T. S. ELIOT

A Dedication to My Wife

To whom I owe the leaping delight
That quickens my senses in our wakingtime
And the rhythm that governs the repose of our sleepingtime,
    The breathing in unison

Of lovers whose bodies smell of each other
Who think the same thoughts without need of speech
And babble the same speech without need of meaning.

No peevish winter wind shall chill
No sullen tropic sun shall wither
The roses in the rose-garden which is ours and ours only

But this dedication is for others to read:
These are private words addressed to you in public.

CHRISTINA ROSSETTI

from *Monna Innominata:*

A Sonnet of Sonnets

IV

I loved you first: but afterwards your love
    Outsoaring mine, sang such a loftier song
As drowned the friendly cooings of my dove.
    Which owes the other most? My love was long,
    And yours one moment seemed to wax more strong;
I loved and guessed at you, you construed me
And loved me for what might or might not be –
    Nay, weights and measures do us both a wrong.
For verily love knows not 'mine' or 'thine';
    With separate 'I' and 'thou' free love has done,
    For one is both and both are one in love:
Rich love knows nought of 'thine that is not mine';
    Both have the strength and both the length thereof,
Both of us, of the love which makes us one.

SEAMUS HEANEY

Scaffolding

Masons, when they start upon a building,
Are careful to test out the scaffolding;

Make sure that planks won't slip at busy points,
Secure all ladders, tighten bolted joints.

And yet all this comes down when the job's done
Showing off walls of sure and solid stone.

So if, my dear, there sometimes seem to be
Old bridges breaking between you and me

Never fear. We may let the scaffolds fall
Confident that we have built our wall.

WILLIAM SHAKESPEARE

Sonnet 29

When, in disgrace with fortune and men's eyes,
I all alone beweep my outcast state,
And trouble deaf heaven with my bootless cries,
And look upon myself and curse my fate,
Wishing me like to one more rich in hope,
Featured like him, like him with friends possessed,
Desiring this man's art and that man's scope,
With what I most enjoy contented least:
Yet in these thoughts myself almost despising,
Haply I think on thee, and then my state,
Like to the lark at break of day arising
From sullen earth, sings hymns at heaven's gate;
   For thy sweet love remembered such wealth brings
   That then I scorn to change my state with kings.

JAMES THOMSON

Gifts

Give a man a horse he can ride,
    Give a man a boat he can sail;
And his rank and wealth, his strength and health,
    On sea nor shore shall fail.

Give a man a pipe he can smoke
    Give a man a book he can read:
And his home is bright with a calm delight,
    Though the room be poor indeed.

Give a man a girl he can love,
    As I, O my love, love thee;
And his heart is great with the pulse of fate,
    At home, on land, on sea.

SAMUEL TAYLOR COLERIDGE

Lines from a Notebook (February 1807)

And in Life's noisiest hour,
　　There whispers still the ceaseless love of thee,
The heart's *self-solace* and soliloquy.

———

You mould my hopes, you fashion me within;
And to the leading love-throb in the heart
Thro' all my being, thro' my pulse's beat;
You lie in all my many thoughts, like light,
Like the fair light of dawn, or summer-eve
On rippling stream, or cloud-reflecting lake.

And looking to the heaven, that bends above you,
How oft I bless the lot, that made me love you.

EMILY DICKINSON

Of all the Souls that stand create –
I have elected – One –
When Sense from Spirit – flies away –
And Subterfuge – is done –
When that which is – and that which was –
Apart – intrinsic – stand –
And this brief Drama in the flesh –
Is shifted – like a Sand –
When Figures show their royal Front –
And Mists – are carved away,
Behold the Atom – I preferred –
To all the lists of Clay!

SIR JOHN DAVIES

If you would know the love which I you bear,
Compare it to the ring which your fair hand
Shall make more precious when you shall it wear:
So my love's nature you shall understand.
Is it of metal pure? So you shall prove
My love, which ne'er disloyal thought did stain.
Hath it no end? So endless is my love,
Unless you it destroy with your disdain.
Doth it the purer wax the more 'tis tried?
So doth my love: yet herein they dissent,
That whereas gold, the more 'tis purified,
By waxing less doth show some part is spent,
My love doth wax more pure by your more trying,
And yet increaseth in the purifying.

RICHARD MONCKTON MILNES, LORD HOUGHTON

from *Love-Thoughts*

IV

Dream no more that grief and pain
Could such hearts as ours enchain,
Safe from loss and safe from gain,
    Free, as love makes free.

When false friends pass coldly by,
Sigh, in earnest pity, sigh,
Turning thine unclouded eye
    Up from them to me.

Hear not danger's trampling feet,
Feel not sorrow's wintry sleet,
Trust that life is just and meet,
    With mine arm round thee.

Lip on lip, and eye to eye,
Love to love, we live, we die;
No more thou, and no more I,
    We, and only we!

WALT WHITMAN

We Two, How Long We Were Fooled

We two, how long we were fooled,
Now transmuted, we swiftly escape as Nature escapes,
We are Nature, long have we been absent, but now we return,
We become plants, trunks, foliage, roots, bark,
We are bedded in the ground, we are rocks,
We are oaks, we grow in the openings side by side,
We browse, we are two among the wild herds spontaneous
      as any,
We are two fishes swimming in the sea together,
We are what locust blossoms are, we drop scent around lanes
      mornings and evenings,
We are also the coarse smut of beasts, vegetables, minerals,
We are two predatory hawks, we soar above and look down,
We are two resplendent suns, we it is who balance ourselves
      orbic and stellar, we are as two comets,
We prowl fanged and four-footed in the woods, we spring
      on prey,
We are two clouds forenoons and afternoons driving overhead,
We are seas mingling, we are two of those cheerful waves rolling
      over each other and interwetting each other,
We are what the atmosphere is, transparent, receptive, pervious,
      impervious,
We are snow, rain, cold, darkness, we are each product and
      influence of the globe,
We have circled and circled till we have arrived home again,
      we two,
We have voided all but freedom and all but our own joy.

A Birthday

My heart is like a singing bird
  Whose nest is in a watered shoot;
My heart is like an apple tree
  Whose boughs are bent with thickset fruit;
My heart is like a rainbow shell
  That paddles in a halcyon sea;
My heart is gladder than all these
  Because my love is come to me.

Raise me a dais of silk and down;
  Hang it with vair and purple dyes;
Carve it in doves and pomegranates,
  And peacocks with a hundred eyes;
Work it in gold and silver grapes,
  In leaves and silver fleurs-de-lys;
Because the birthday of my life
  Is come, my love is come to me.

WILLIAM CARTWRIGHT

from *To Chloe,*

Who Wished Herself Young Enough for Me

There are two births, the one when light
   First strikes the new awakened sense;
The other when two souls unite;
   And we must count our life from thence:
When you loved me, and I loved you,
Then both of us were born anew.

Love then to us did new souls give,
   And in those souls did plant new powers;
Since when another life we live,
   The breath we breathe is his, not ours;
Love makes those young, whom age doth chill,
And whom he finds young, keeps young still.

CHRISTOPHER BRENNAN

Because She Would Ask Me Why I Loved Her

If questioning could make us wise
no eyes would ever gaze in eyes;
if all our tale were told in speech
no mouths would wander each to each.

Were spirits free from mortal mesh
and love not bound in hearts of flesh
no aching breasts would yearn to meet
and find their ecstasy complete.

For who is there that lives and knows
the secret powers by which he grows?
Were knowledge all, what were our need
to thrill and faint and sweetly bleed?

Then seek not, sweet, the *If* and *Why*
I love you now until I die:
For I must love because I live
And life in me is what you give.

ELIZABETH BARRETT BROWNING

from *Sonnets from the Portuguese*

XLIII

How do I love thee? Let me count the ways –
I love thee to the depth and breadth & height
My soul can reach, when feeling out of sight
For the ends of Being and Ideal Grace.
I love thee to the level of every day's
Most quiet need, by sun and candlelight –
I love thee freely, as men strive for Right, –
I love thee purely, as they turn from Praise;
I love thee with a passion, put to use
In my old griefs, and with my childhood's faith:
I love thee with a love I seemed to lose
With my lost Saints, – I love thee with the breath,
Smiles, tears, of all my life! – and, if God choose,
I shall but love thee better after my death.

EDMUND SPENSER

from *Amoretti*

LXXII

Oft when my spirit doth spread her bolder wings,
    in mind to mount up to the purest sky:
    it down is weighed with thought of earthly things
    and clogged with burden of mortality,
Where when that sovereign beauty it doth spy,
    resembling heaven's glory in her light:
    drawn with sweet pleasure's bait, it back doth fly,
    and unto heaven forgets her former flight.
There my frail fancy fed with full delight,
    doth bathe in bliss and mantleth most at ease:
    ne thinks of other heaven, but how it might
    her heart's desire with most contentment please.
Heart need not wish none other happiness,
    but here on earth to have such heaven's bliss.

W. B. YEATS

He Wishes for the Cloths of Heaven

Had I the heavens' embroidered cloths,
Enwrought with golden and silver light,
The blue and the dim and the dark cloths
Of night and light and the half-light,
I would spread the cloths under your feet:
But, I being poor, have only my dreams;
I have spread my dreams under your feet;
Tread softly because you tread on my dreams.

Marriage Morning

Light, so low upon earth,
   You send a flash to the sun.
Here is the golden close of love,
   All my wooing is done.
Oh, the woods and the meadows,
   Woods where we hid from the wet,
Stiles where we stayed to be kind,
   Meadows in which we met!

Light, so low in the vale
   You flash and lighten afar,
For this is the golden morning of love,
   And you are his morning star.
Flash, I am coming, I come,
   By meadow and stile and wood,
Oh, lighten into my eyes and heart,
   Into my heart and my blood!

Heart, are you great enough
   For a love that never tires?
O heart, are you great enough for love?
   I have heard of thorns and briers.
Over the thorns and briers,
   Over the meadow and stiles,
Over the world to the end of it
   Flash for a million miles.

somewhere i have never travelled,gladly beyond
any experience,your eyes have their silence:
in your most frail gesture are things which enclose me,
or which i cannot touch because they are too near

your slightest look easily will unclose me
though i have closed myself as fingers,
you open always petal by petal myself as Spring opens
(touching skilfully,mysteriously)her first rose

or if your wish be to close me, i and
my life will shut very beautifully,suddenly,
as when the heart of this flower imagines
the snow carefully everywhere descending;

nothing which we are to perceive in this world equals
the power of your intense fragility:whose texture
compels me with the colour of its countries,
rendering death and forever with each breathing

(i do not know what it is about you that closes
and opens;only something in me understands
the voice of your eyes is deeper than all roses)
nobody,not even the rain,has such small hands

BRIAN PATTEN

Her Song

For no other reason than I love him wholly
I am here; for this one night at least
The world has shrunk to a boyish breast
On which my head, brilliant and exhausted, rests,
And can know of nothing more complete.

Let the dawn assemble all its guilts, its worries
And small doubts that, but for love, would infect
This perfect heart.
I am as far beyond doubt as the sun.
I am as far beyond doubt as is possible.

Promises

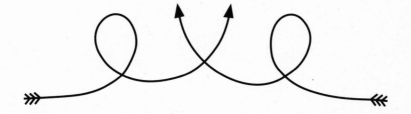

E. J. SCOVELL

A Betrothal

Put your hand on my heart, say that you love me as
The woods upon the hills cleave to the hills' contours.

I will uphold you, trunk and shoot and flowering sheaf,
And I will hold you, roots and fruit and fallen leaf.

ROBERT BURNS

Song

Come, let me take thee to my breast,
   And pledge we ne'er shall sunder;
And I shall spurn, as vilest dust,
   The world's wealth and grandeur:
And do I hear my Jeanie own
   That equal transports move her?
I ask for dearest life alone
   That I may live to love her.

Thus, in my arms, wi' a' thy charms,
   I clasp my countless treasure;
I'll seek nae mair o' Heaven to share,
   Than sic a moment's pleasure:
And by thy een, sae bonie blue,
   I swear I'm thine for ever!
And on thy lips I seal my vow,
   And break it shall I never!

een eyes

SARA TEASDALE

I Would Live in Your Love

I would live in your love as the sea-grasses live in the sea,
Borne up by each wave as it passes, drawn down by each
   wave that recedes;
I would empty my soul of the dreams that have gathered in me,
I would beat with your heart as it beats, I would follow your
   soul as it leads.

i carry your heart with me(i carry it in
my heart)i am never without it(anywhere
i go you go,my dear;and whatever is done
by only me is your doing,my darling)
                                        i fear
no fate(for you are my fate, my sweet)i want
no world(for beautiful you are my world,my true)
and it's you are whatever a moon has always meant
and whatever a sun will always sing is you

here is the deepest secret nobody knows
(here is the root of the root and the bud of the bud
and the sky of the sky of a tree called life;which grows
higher than soul can hope or mind can hide)
and this is the wonder that's keeping the stars apart

i carry your heart(i carry it in my heart)

THE KING JAMES BIBLE

from *The Song of Solomon*

I am my beloved's, and his desire is towards me.

Come, my beloved, let us go forth into the field; let us lodge in the villages.

Let us get up early to the vineyards; let us see if the vine flourish, whether the tender grapes appear, and the pomegranates bud forth: there I will give thee my loves.

The mandrakes give a smell, and at our gates are all manner of pleasant fruits, new and old, which I have laid up for thee, O my beloved.

[. . .]

Set me as a seal upon thine heart, as a seal upon thy arm: for love is strong as death; jealousy is cruel as the grave: the coals thereof are coals of fire, which hath a most vehement flame.

Many waters cannot quench love, neither can the floods drown it: if a man would give all the substance of his house for love, it would be utterly contemned.

MIMI KHALVATI

Ghazal

If I am the grass and you the breeze, blow through me.
If I am the rose and you the bird, then woo me.

If you are the rhyme and I the refrain, don't hang
on my lips, come and I'll come too when you cue me.

If yours is the iron fist in the velvet glove
when the arrow flies, the heart is pierced, tattoo me.

If mine is the venomous tongue, the serpent's tail,
charmer, use your charm, weave a spell and subdue me.

If I am the laurel leaf in your crown, you are
the arms around my bark, arms that never knew me.

Oh would that I were bark! So old and still in leaf.
And you, dropping in my shade, dew to bedew me!

What shape should I take to marry your own, have you –
hawk to my shadow, moth to my flame – pursue me?

If I rise in the east as you die in the west,
die for my sake, my love, every night renew me.

If, when it ends, we are just good friends, be my Friend,
muse, lover and guide, Shamsuddin to my Rumi.

Be heaven and earth to me and I'll be twice the me
I am, if only half the world you are to me.

ANONYMOUS

I will give my love an apple without e'er a core,
I will give my love a house without e'er a door,
I will give my love a palace wherein she may be,
And she may unlock it without any key.

My head is the apple without e'er a core,
My mind is the house without e'er a door,
My heart is the palace wherein she may be,
And she may unlock it without any key.

NORMAN MACCAIG

Sure proof

I can no more describe you
than I can put a thing for the first time
where it already is.

If I could make a ladder of light
or comb the hair of a dream girl with a real comb
or pour a table into a jug . . .

I'm not good at impossible things.
And that is why I'm sure
I will love you for my ever.

GEORGE GASCOIGNE

That self-same tongue which first did thee entreat
To link thy liking with my lucky love,
That trusty tongue must now these words repeat:
I love thee still, my fancy cannot move.
That dreadless heart which durst attempt the thought
To win thy will with mine for to consent
Maintains that vow which love in me first wrought:
I love thee still, and never shall repent.
That happy hand which hardily did touch,
Thy tender body to my deep delight
Shall serve with sword to prove my passion such
As loves thee still, much more than it can write.
       Thus love I still with tongue, hand, heart and all,
       And when I change, let vengeance on me fall.

AMY LOWELL

To a Friend

I ask but one thing of you, only one.
That you will always be my dream of you;
That never shall I wake to find untrue
All this I have believed and rested on,
Forever vanished, like a vision gone
Out into the night. Alas, how few
There are who strike in us a chord we knew
Existed, but so seldom heard its tone
We tremble at the half-forgotten sound.
The world is full of rude awakenings
And heaven-born castles shattered to the ground,
Yet still our human longing vainly clings
To a belief in beauty through all wrongs.
O stay your hand, and leave my heart its songs!

JOHN DOWLAND

Dear, if you change, I'll never choose again;
Sweet, if you shrink, I'll never think of love;
Fair, if you fail, I'll judge all beauty vain;
Wise, if too weak, more wits I'll never prove.
     Dear, sweet, fair, wise, change, shrink, nor be not weak;
     And, on my faith, my faith shall never break.

Earth with her flowers shall sooner heaven adorn;
Heaven her bright stars, through earth's dim globe shall move;
Fire, heat shall lose; and frosts of flames be born;
Air made to shine, as black as hell shall prove:
     Earth, heaven, fire, air, the world transformed shall view,
     Ere I prove false to faith or strange to you.

So in Love

Strange dear, but true, dear,
When I'm close to you, dear,
The stars fill the sky,
So in love with you am I.
Even without you
My arms fold about you,
You know, darling, why,
So in love with you am I.
In love with the night mysterious
The night when you first were there,
In love with my joy delirious
When I knew that you could care.
So taunt me and hurt me,
Deceive me, desert me,
I'm yours 'til I die . . .
So in love,
So in love,
So in love with you, my love, am I.

I

One word is too often profaned
   For me to profane it,
One feeling too falsely disdained
   For thee to disdain it;
One hope is too like despair
   For prudence to smother,
And pity from thee more dear
   Than that from another.

II

I can give not what men call love,
   But wilt thou accept not
The worship the heart lifts above
   And the heavens reject not, –
The desire of the moth for the star,
   Of the night for the morrow,
The devotion to something afar
   From the sphere of our sorrow?

EDITH WHARTON

from *The Mortal Lease*

V

Yet for one rounded moment I will be
No more to you than what my lips may give,
And in the circle of your kisses live
As in some island of a storm-blown sea,
Where the cold surges of infinity
Upon the outward reefs unheeded grieve,
And the loud murmur of our blood shall weave
Primeval silences round you and me.

If in that moment we are all we are,
We live enough. Let this for all requite.
Do I not know, some wingèd things from far
Are borne along illimitable night
To dance their lives out in a single flight
Between the moonrise and the setting star?

Is it for now or for always,
The world hangs on a stalk?
Is it a trick or a trysting-place,
The woods we have found to walk?

Is it a mirage or miracle,
Your lips that lift at mine:
And the suns like a juggler's juggling-balls,
Are they a sham or a sign?

Shine out, my sudden angel,
Break fear with breast and brow,
I take you now and for always,
For always is always now.

How like a fire doth love increase in me,
The longer that it lasts, the stronger still,
The greater, purer, brighter, and doth fill
No eye with wonder more; then hopes still be

Bred in my breast, where fires of love are free
To use that part to their best pleasing will,
And now impossible it is to kill
The heat so great where Love his strength doth see.

Mine eyes can scarce sustain the flames, my heart
Doth trust in them my longings to impart,
And languishingly strive to show my love;

My breath not able is to breathe least part
Of that increasing fuel of my smart;
Yet love I will till I but ashes prove.

ROBERT HERRICK

To Anthea,

Who May Command Him Any Thing

Bid me to live, and I will live
  Thy Protestant to be;
Or bid me love, and I will give
  A loving heart to thee.

A heart as soft, a heart as kind,
  A heart as sound and free
As in the whole world thou canst find,
  That heart I'll give to thee.

Bid that heart stay, and it will stay
  To honour thy decree:
Or bid it languish quite away,
  And't shall do so for thee.

Bid me to weep, and I will weep
  While I have eyes to see:
And, having none, yet will I keep
  A heart to weep for thee.

Bid me despair, and I'll despair
  Under that cypress tree:
Or bid me die, and I will dare
  Even death, to die for thee.

Thou art my life, my love, my heart,
  The very eyes of me:
And hast command of every part,
  To live and die for thee.

EDNA ST VINCENT MILLAY

from *Fatal Interview*

XXX

Love is not all: it is not meat nor drink
Nor slumber nor a roof against the rain;
Nor yet a floating spar to men that sink
And rise and sink and rise and sink again;
Love can not fill the thickened lung with breath,
Nor clean the blood, nor set the fractured bone;
Yet many a man is making friends with death
Even as I speak, for lack of love alone.
It well may be that in a difficult hour,
Pinned down by pain and moaning for release,
Or nagged by want past resolution's power,
I might be driven to sell your love for peace,
Or trade the memory of this night for food.
It well may be. I do not think I would.

ROBERT GRAVES

Whole Love

Every choice is always the wrong choice,
Every vote cast is always cast away –
How can truth hover between alternatives?

Then love me more than dearly, love me wholly,
Love me with no weighing of circumstance,
As I am pledged in honour to love you:

With no weakness, with no speculation
On what might happen should you and I prove less
Than bringers-to-be of our own certainty.
Neither was born by hazard: each foreknew
The extreme possession we are grown into.

LYNETTE ROBERTS

Green Madrigal [I]

Peace, my stranger is a tree
Growing naturally through all its
Discomforts, trials and emergencies
Of growth.
It is green and resolved
It breathes with anguish
Yet it releases peace, peace of mind
Growth, movement.
It walks this greening sweetness
Throughout all the earth,
Where sky and sun tender its habits
As I would yours.

ROBERT BURNS

A Red, Red Rose

My luve is like a red, red rose,
  That's newly sprung in June:
My luve is like the melodie,
  That's sweetly play'd in tune.
As fair art thou, my bonie lass,
  So deep in luve am I,
And I will luve thee still, my dear,
  Till a' the seas gang dry.

Till a' the seas gang dry, my dear,
  And the rocks melt wi' the sun!
And I will luve thee still, my dear,
  While the sands o' life shall run.
And fare-thee-weel, my only luve,
  And fare-thee-weel a while!
And I will come again, my luve,
  Tho' it were ten thousand mile.

ROBERT LOUIS STEVENSON

from *Songs of Travel*

XI

I will make you brooches and toys for your delight
Of bird-song at morning and star-shine at night.
I will make a palace fit for you and me
Of green days in forests and blue days at sea.

I will make my kitchen, and you shall keep your room,
Where white flows the river and bright blows the broom,
And you shall wash your linen and keep your body white
In rainfall at morning and dewfall at night.

And this shall be for music when no one else is near,
The fine song for singing, the rare song to hear!
That only I remember, that only you admire,
Of the broad road that stretches and the roadside fire.

JOSHUA SYLVESTER

Were I as base as is the lowly plain,
And you, my Love, as high as heaven above,
Yet should the thoughts of me, your humble swain,
Ascend to heaven in honour of my love.
Were I as high as heaven above plain,
And you, my Love, as humble and as low
As are the deepest bottoms of the main,
Whereso'er you were, with you my love should go.
Were you the earth, dear Love, and I the skies,
My love should shine on you like to the sun,
And look upon you with ten thousand eyes
Till heaven waxed blind, and till the world were done.
Whereso'er I am, below, or else above you,
Whereso'er you are, my heart shall truly love you.

EDNA ST VINCENT MILLAY

Modern Declaration

I, having loved ever since I was a child a few things, never having
    wavered
In these affections; never through shyness in the houses of the rich
    or in the presence of clergymen having denied these loves;
Never when worked upon by cynics like chiropractors having
    grunted or clicked a vertebra to the discredit of these loves;
Never when anxious to land a job having diminished them by a
    conniving smile; or when befuddled by drink
Jeered at them through heartache or lazily fondled the fingers of
    their alert enemies; declare

That I shall love you always.
No matter what party is in power;
No matter what temporarily expedient combination of allied
    interests wins the war;
Shall love you always.

Vow

I vow to honour the commitment made this day
Which, unlike the flowers and the cake,
Will not wither or decay. A promise, not to obey
But to respond joyfully, to forgive and to console,
For once incomplete, we now are whole.

I vow to bear in mind that if, at times,
Things seem to go from bad to worse
They also go from bad to better.
The lost purse is handed in, the letter
Contains wonderful news. Trains run on time,
Hurricanes run out of breath, floods subside,
And toast lands jam-side up.

And with this ring, my final vow:
To recall, whatever the future may bring,
The love I feel for you now.

Hinterhof

Stay near to me and I'll stay near to you –
As near as you are dear to me will do,
    Near as the rainbow to the rain,
    The west wind to the windowpane,
As fire to the hearth, as dawn to dew.

Stay true to me and I'll stay true to you –
As true as you are new to me will do,
    New as the rainbow in the spray,
    Utterly new in every way,
New in the way that what you say is true.

Stay near to me, stay true to me. I'll stay
As near, as true to you as heart could pray.
    Heart never hoped that one might be
    Half of the things you are to me –
The dawn, the fire, the rainbow and the day.

ELIZABETH GARRETT

Epithalamium

Ask not, this night, how we shall love
When we are three-year lovers;
How clothes, as lapsing tides, as love,
May slide, three summers over;
Nor ask when the eye's quick darknesses
Throw shadows on our skin
How we shall know our nakedness
In the difference of things.

Ask not whose salty hand turns back
The sea's sheet on the shore,
Or how the split and broken moon rides
Still each wave's humped back –
Ask not, for it is given as my pledge
That night shall be our sole inquisitor,
Day our respondent, and each parting as the bride
And groom, an hour before their marriage.

ROBERT HERRICK

A Ring Presented to Julia

Julia, I bring
To thee this ring,
Made for thy finger fit;
To show by this,
That our love is
(Or should be) like to it.

Close though it be,
The joint is free:
So, when Love's yoke is on,
It must not gall,
Or fret at all
With hard oppression.

But it must play
Still either way;
And be, too, such a yoke,
As not too wide
To over-slide;
Or be so straight to choke.

So we, who bear
This beam, must rear
Ourselves to such a height:
As that the stay
Of either may
Create the burden light.

And as this round
Is nowhere found
To flaw, or else to sever:
So let our love
As endless prove;
And pure as gold for ever.

JOHN KEATS

Bright star! would I were steadfast as thou art –
   Not in lone splendour hung aloft the night
And watching, with eternal lids apart,
   Like nature's patient, sleepless Eremite,
The moving waters at their priestlike task
   Of pure ablution round earth's human shores,
Or gazing on the new soft-fallen mask
   Of snow upon the mountains and the moors –
No – yet still steadfast, still unchangeable,
   Pillowed upon my fair love's ripening breast,
To feel for ever its soft swell and fall,
   Awake for ever in a sweet unrest,
Still, still to hear her tender-taken breath,
And so live ever – or else swoon to death.

ANNE MACLEOD

There will be no end

There will be no end to the joy, my love.
We will stand together as the stars
sweep the Cuillin, rounding into morning
the bright new morning of the tender heart.
And where we sing, the song will be a fine one
and where we dance, our steps will never fail
to tap the spring of life, of love and laughter
timeless as stars, the wheeling, circling stars
that dance and sing, and sing and dance again:
and there will be no end
to the joy.

Celebrations

PETER MEINKE

The First Marriage

(for Gretchen and Herb: June 15, 1991)

imagine the very first marriage a girl
and boy trembling with some inchoate
need for ceremony a desire for witness:
inventing formality like a wheel or a hoe

in a lost language in a clearing too far from here
a prophet or a prophetess intoned to the lovers
who knelt with their hearts cresting
like the unnamed ocean thinking *This is true*

thinking they will never be alone again
though planets slip their tracks and fish
desert the sea repeating those magic sounds
meaning *I do* on this stone below
this tree before these friends *yes* in body
and word my darkdream my sunsong yes *I do I do*

from *Paradise Lost,* Book IV

Hail, wedded love, mysterious law, true source
Of human offspring, sole propriety
In Paradise of all things common else.
By thee adulterous lust was driven from men
Among the bestial herds to range, by thee
Founded in reason, loyal, just and pure,
Relations dear, and all the charities
Of father, son and brother first were known.
Far be it, that I should write thee sin or blame,
Or think thee unbefitting holiest place,
Perpetual fountain of domestic sweets,
Whose bed is undefiled and chaste pronounced,
Present or past, as saints and patriarchs used.
Here Love his golden shafts employs, here lights
His constant lamp, and waves his purple wings,
Reigns here and revels; not in the bought smile
Of harlots, loveless, joyless, unendeared,
Casual fruition, nor in court amours,
Mixed dance or wanton mask or midnight ball
Or serenade, which the starved lover sings
To his proud fair, best quitted with disdain.
These lulled by nightingales embracing slept,
And on their naked limbs the flowery roof
Showered roses, which the morn repaired. Sleep on,
Blest pair; and O yet happiest if ye seek
No happier state, and know to know no more.

Wreath for a Bridal

What though green leaves only witness
Such pact as is made once only; what matter
That owl voice sole 'yes', while cows utter
Low moos of approve; let sun surpliced in brightness
Stand stock still to laud these mated ones
Whose stark act all coming double luck joins.

Couched daylong in cloisters of stinging nettle
They lie, cut-grass assaulting each separate sense
With savor; coupled so, pure paragons of constance,
This pair seek single state from that dual battle.
Now speak some sacrament to parry scruple
For wedlock wrought within love's proper chapel.

Call here with flying colors all watchful birds
To people the twigged aisles; lead babel tongues
Of animals to choir: 'Look what thresh of wings
Wields guard of honor over these!' Starred with words
Let night bless that luck-rooted mead of clover
Where, bedded like angels, two burn one in fever.

From this holy day on, all pollen blown
Shall strew broadcast so rare a seed on wind
That every breath, thus teeming, set the land
Sprouting fruit, flowers, children most fair in legion
To slay spawn of dragon's teeth: speaking this promise,
Let flesh be knit, and each step hence go famous.

WILLIAM SHAKESPEARE

Sonnet 55

Not marble nor the gilded monuments
Of princes shall outlive this powerful rhyme,
But you shall shine more bright in these contents
Than unswept stone besmeared with sluttish time.
When wasteful war shall statues overturn,
And broils root out the work of masonry,
Nor Mars his sword nor war's quick fire shall burn
The living record of your memory.
'Gainst death and all oblivious enmity
Shall you pace forth; your praise shall still find room
Even in the eyes of all posterity
That wear this world out to the ending doom.
  So, till the judgment that yourself arise,
   You live in this, and dwell in lovers' eyes.

ELIZABETH JENNINGS

Love Poem

There is a shyness that we have
Only with those whom we most love.
Something it has to do also
With how we cannot bring to mind
A face whose every line we know.
O love is kind, O love is kind.

That there should still remain the first
Sweetness, also the later thirst –
This is why pain must play some part
In all true feelings that we find
And every shaking of the heart.
O love is kind, O love is kind.

And it is right that we should want
Discretion, secrecy, no hint
Of what we share. Love which cries out,
And wants the world to understand,
Is love that holds itself in doubt.
For love is quiet, and love is kind.

JAMES MCAULEY

One Thing at Least

One thing at least I understood
Practically from the start,
That loving must be learnt by heart
If it's to be any good.

It isn't in the flash of thunder,
But in the silent power to give –
A habit into which we live
Ourselves, and grow to be a wonder.

Some like me are slow to learn:
What's plain can be mysterious still.
Feelings alter, fade, return,

But love stands constant in the will:
It's not alone the touching, seeing,
It's how to mean the other's being.

RICHARD EDES

Of Man and Wife

No love to love of man and wife;
No hope to hope of constant heart;
No joy to joy in wedded life;
No faith to faith in either part:
Flesh is of flesh, and bone of bone
When deeds and words and thoughts are one.

Thy friend an other friend may be,
But other self is not the same;
Thy spouse the self-same is with thee,
In body, mind, in goods and name:
No thine, no mine, may other call,
For all is one, and one is all.

Sonnet 116

Let me not to the marriage of true minds
Admit impediments. Love is not love
Which alters when it alteration finds,
Or bends with the remover to remove.
O no, it is an ever-fixèd mark
That looks on tempests and is never shaken;
It is the star to every wandering bark,
Whose worth's unknown, although his height be taken.
Love's not Time's fool, though rosy lips and cheeks
Within his bending sickle's compass come;
Love alters not with his brief hours and weeks,
But bears it out even to the edge of doom.
    If this be error and upon me proved,
    I never writ, nor no man ever loved.

JOHN FORD

A Bridal Song

from The Broken Heart

Comforts lasting, loves increasing,
Like soft hours never ceasing;
Plenty's pleasure, peace complying,
Without jars, or tongues envying;
Hearts by holy union wedded,
More than theirs by custom bedded;
Fruitful issues; life so graced,
Not by age to be defaced,
Budding, as the year ensu'th,
Every spring another youth:
All what thought can add beside,
Crown this bridegroom and this bride!

Nuptials

River, be their teacher,
that together they may turn
their future highs and lows
into one hopeful flow

Two opposite shores
feeding from a single source.

Mountain, be their milestone,
that hand in hand they rise above
familiarity's worn tracks
into horizons of their own

Two separate footpaths
dreaming of a common peak.

Birdsong, be their mantra,
that down the frail aisles of their days,
their twilight hearts twitter morning
and their dreams prove branch enough.

CHRISTINA ROSSETTI

Song

Two doves upon the selfsame branch,
  Two lilies on a single stem,
Two butterflies upon one flower: –
  Oh happy they who look on them.

Who look upon them hand in hand
  Flushed in the rosy summer light;
Who look upon them hand in hand
  And never give a thought to night.

ROBERT FROST

The Master Speed

No speed of wind or water rushing by
But you have speed far greater. You can climb
Back up a stream of radiance to the sky,
And back through history up the stream of time.
And you were given this swiftness, not for haste
Nor chiefly that you may go where you will,
But in the rush of everything to waste,
That you may have the power of standing still –
Off any still or moving thing you say.
Two such as you with such a master speed
Cannot be parted nor be swept away
From one another once you are agreed
That life is only life forevermore
Together wing to wing and oar to oar.

RICHARD MEIER

Moment

That moment in a wedding –
the sense of cresting, as the goodwill wells –

say one could translate that into sight
you'd see, perhaps, two people side by side –

there in the newfound centre of the world –
in front of them a mirror and one more behind

in which they find themselves reflected first themselves

then all the couples who have stood as frank as they do –
all the marrying kind – arranged along

love's entire length in one pulsating line
that, captured in the language of the heart,

feels like a cresting, as the goodwill wells –
that moment in a wedding.

JANE HOLLAND

They Are a Tableau at the Kissing-Gate

Maids of honour, bridegroom, bride,
the best man in a grey silk suit,
a flash to catch them in the arching
stone, confettied by a sudden gust –
an apple tree in full white spread
beyond the reach of bone and dust.

I am the driver in a passing car:
the wedding dress a cloud of lace.
A small hand clutching at a skirt,
some nervous bridesmaid, eight
or maybe nine years old, has seen
the blossom fall, has closed her eyes –

her head falls back into the scent,
the soundless whirr and whirl of earth-
bound petals, like sycamore seeds
on a current of air, silent helicopters
bringing light – a wedding-gift
the bride will brush away, unconsciously.

This is no ordinary act, no summer fête,
another simple wedding held in June.
This is the wind shaking the apple tree,
the bell above the kissing-gate,
the sudden fall of blossom into light
which only love and innocence can see.

We must be held accountable to love:
where they step out together arm in arm
as newly-weds, spring-cleaned, and climb
into a waiting car beneath a summer sky,
the blossom will still fall, unstoppable –
a drift of change across a changeless time.

JOHN CLARE

A Spring Morning

The Spring comes in with all her hues and smells,
In freshness breathing over hills and dells;
O'er woods where May her gorgeous drapery flings,
And meads washed fragrant by their laughing springs.
Fresh are new-opened flowers, untouched and free
From the bold rifling of the amorous bee.
The happy time of singing birds is come,
And love's lone pilgrimage now finds a home;
Among the mossy oaks now coos the dove,
And the hoarse crow finds softer notes for love.
The foxes play around their dens and bark
In joy's excess, mid woodland shadows dark.
The flowers join lips below, the leaves above;
And every sound that meets the ear is love.

ADRIAN HENRI

Love is . . .

Love is feeling cold in the back of vans
Love is a fanclub with only two fans
Love is walking holding paintstained hands
Love is

Love is fish and chips on winter nights
Love is blankets full of strange delights
Love is when you don't put out the light
Love is

Love is the presents in Christmas shops
Love is when you're feeling Top of the Pops
Love is what happens when the music stops
Love is

Love is white panties lying all forlorn
Love is pink nightdresses still slightly warm
Love is when you have to leave at dawn
Love is

Love is you and love is me
Love is prison and love is free
Love's what's there when you are away from me
Love is . . .

WILLIAM MORRIS

from *Love is Enough*

Love is enough: though the World be a-waning,
And the woods have no voice but the voice of complaining,
  Though the sky be too dark for dim eyes to discover
The gold-cups and daisies fair blooming thereunder,
Though the hills be held shadows, and the sea a dark wonder,
  And this day draw a veil over all deeds passed over,
Yet their hands shall not tremble, their feet shall not falter;
The void shall not weary, the fear shall not alter
  These lips and these eyes of the loved and the lover.

SAMUEL TAYLOR COLERIDGE

Answer to a Child's Question

Do you ask what the birds say? The Sparrow, the Dove,
The Linnet and Thrush say, 'I love and I love!'
In the winter they're silent – the wind is so strong;
What it says, I don't know, but it sings a loud song.
But green leaves, and blossoms, and sunny warm weather,
And singing, and loving – all come back together.
But the lark is so brimful of gladness and love,
The green fields below him, the blue sky above,
That he sings, and he sings; and for ever sings he –
'I love my Love, and my Love loves me!'

LIZ LOCHHEAD

Epithalamium

for Joe and Annie Thomson

For marriage, love and love alone's the argument.
Sweet ceremony, then hand-in-hand we go
Taking to our changed, still dangerous days, our complement.
We think we know ourselves, but all we know
Is: love surprises us. It's like when sunlight flings
A sudden shaft that lights up glamorous the rain
Across a Glasgow street – or when Botanic Spring's
First crisp, dry breath turns February air champagne.

Delight's infectious – your quotidian friends
Put on, with gladrag finery today, your joy,
Renew in themselves the right true ends
They won't let old griefs, old lives, destroy.
When at our lover's feet our opened selves we've laid
We find ourselves, and all the world, remade.

from *Endymion:*
A Poetic Romance,
Book I

A thing of beauty is a joy for ever:
Its loveliness increases; it will never
Pass into nothingness; but still will keep
A bower quiet for us, and a sleep
Full of sweet dreams, and health, and quiet breathing.
Therefore, on every morrow, are we wreathing
A flowery band to bind us to the earth,
Spite of despondence, of the inhuman dearth
Of noble natures, of the gloomy days,
Of all the unhealthy and o'er-darkened ways
Made for our searching: yes, in spite of all,
Some shape of beauty moves away the pall
From our dark spirits. Such the sun, the moon,
Trees old, and young, sprouting a shady boon
For simple sheep; and such are daffodils
With the green world they live in; and clear rills
That for themselves a cooling covert make
'Gainst the hot season; the mid forest brake,
Rich with a sprinkling of fair musk-rose blooms:
And such too is the grandeur of the dooms
We have imagined for the mighty dead;
All lovely tales that we have heard or read –
An endless fountain of immortal drink,
Pouring unto us from the heaven's brink.

from *The Song of Hiawatha*

XI

HIAWATHA'S WEDDING-FEAST

Sumptuous was the feast Nokomis
Made at Hiawatha's wedding;
All the bowls were made of bass-wood,
White and polished very smoothly,
All the spoons of horn of bison,
Black and polished very smoothly.

She had sent through all the village
Messengers with wands of willow,
As a sign of invitation,
As a token of the feasting;
And the wedding guests assembled,
Clad in all their richest raiment,
Robes of fur and belts of wampum,
Splendid with their paint and plumage,
Beautiful with beads and tassels.

First they ate the sturgeon, Nahma,
And the pike, the Maskenozha,
Caught and cooked by old Nokomis;
Then on pemican they feasted,
Pemican and buffalo marrow,
Haunch of deer and hump of bison,
Yellow cakes of the Mondamin,
And the wild rice of the river.

But the gracious Hiawatha,
And the lovely Laughing Water,
And the careful old Nokomis,
Tasted not the food before them,
Only waited on the others,
Only served their guests in silence.

And when all the guests had finished,
Old Nokomis, brisk and busy,
From an ample pouch of otter,
Filled the red-stone pipes for smoking
With tobacco from the South-land,
Mixed with bark of the red willow,
And with herbs and leaves of fragrance.

RICHARD WILBUR

A Wedding Toast

(M.C.H., C.H.W., 14 July 1971)

St John tells how, at Cana's wedding feast,
The water-pots poured wine in such amount
That by his sober count
There were a hundred gallons at the least.

It made no earthly sense, unless to show
How whatsoever love elects to bless
Brims to a sweet excess
That can without depletion overflow.

Which is to say that what love sees is true;
That this world's fullness is not made but found.
Life hungers to abound
And pour its plenty out for such as you.

Now, if your loves will lend an ear to mine,
I toast you both, good son and dear new daughter.
May you not lack for water,
And may that water smack of Cana's wine.

Carry her over the water,
    And set her down under the tree,
Where the culvers white all day and all night,
    And the winds from every quarter,
Sing agreeably, agreeably, agreeably of love.

Put a gold ring on her finger,
    And press her close to your heart,
While the fish in the lake snapshots take,
    And the frog, that sanguine singer,
Sings agreeably, agreeably, agreeably of love.

The streets shall all flock to your marriage,
    The houses turn round to look,
The tables and chairs say suitable prayers,
    And the horses drawing your carriage
Sing agreeably, agreeably, agreeably of love.

The Owl and the Pussy-Cat

The Owl and the Pussy-cat went to sea
  In a beautiful pea-green boat,
They took some honey, and plenty of money,
  Wrapped up in a five-pound note.
The Owl looked up to the stars above,
  And sang to a small guitar,
'O lovely Pussy! O Pussy, my love,
  What a beautiful Pussy you are,
      You are,
      You are!
What a beautiful Pussy you are!'

Pussy said to the Owl, 'You elegant fowl!
  How charmingly sweet you sing!
O let us be married! too long we have tarried:
  But what shall we do for a ring?'
They sailed away, for a year and a day,
  To the land where the Bong-tree grows,

And there in a wood a Piggy-wig stood,
   With a ring at the end of his nose,
         His nose,
         His nose,
With a ring at the end of his nose.

'Dear Pig, are you willing to sell for one shilling
   Your ring?' Said the Piggy, 'I will.'
So they took it away, and were married next day
   By the Turkey who lives on the hill.
They dined on mince, and slices of quince,
   Which they ate with a runcible spoon;
And hand in hand, on the edge of the sand,
   They danced by the light of the moon,
         The moon,
         The moon,
They danced by the light of the moon.

ANONYMOUS

Love Will Find Out the Way

Over the mountains
And over the waves,
Under the fountains
And under the graves;
Under floods that are the deepest
Which Neptune obey,
Over rocks that are steepest,
Love will find out the way.

Where there is no place
For the glow-worm to lie,
Where there is no space
For receipt of a fly;
Where the midge dares not venture
Lest herself fast she lay,
But if Love come, he will enter
And will find out the way.

Some think to lose him
By having him confined;
And some do suppose him,
Poor heart! to be blind;
But if never so close you wall him,
Do the best that you may,
Blind Love, if so you call him,
Will find out his way.

You may train the eagle
To stoop to your fist;
Or you may inveigle
The phoenix of the east,
The lioness, you may move her
To give over her prey;
But you'll never stop a lover:
He will find out his way.

If the earth it should part him,
He would gallop it over;
If the seas should overthwart him,
He would swim to the shore;
Should his love become a swallow,
Through the air to stray,
Love will lend wings to follow,
And will find out the way.

There is no striving
To cross his intent;
There is no contriving
His plots to prevent;
But if once the message greet him
That his true love doth stay,
If death should come and meet him
Love will find out the way.

KATE CLANCHY

For a Wedding

(Camilla and Kieran 9/8/94)

Cousin, I think the shape of a marriage
is like the shelves my parents have carried
through Scotland to London, three houses;

is not distinguished, fine, French-polished,
but plywood and tatty, made
in the first place for children to batter,

still carrying markings in green felt tip,
but always, where there are books
and a landing, managing to fit;

that marriage has lumps like
their button-backed sofa, constantly;
shortly, about to be stuffed;

and that love grows fat
as their squinting cat, swelling
round as a loaf from her basket.

I wish you years that shape, that form,
and a pond in a Sunday, urban garden;
where you'll see your joined reflection tremble,

stand and watch the waterboatmen
skate with ease across the surface tension.

GEOFFREY CHAUCER

from *The Franklin's Tale*

from *The Canterbury Tales*

For one thing, sirs, I confidently say:
In friendship, one another must obey,
If they should hope to keep in company;
True love is not constrained by mastery.
When mastery comes, the God of Love departs;
He beats his winds and leaves those sundered hearts!
For love's a thing, like any spirit: free.
Of course all women love their liberty,
And would not be constrained or made a slave –
And so do men their independence crave.
Observe how he who has most patience finds
Advantage in affairs of hearts or minds:
This patience is a potent virtue, for
It vanquishes, as men have said before,
Those things which rigour never may achieve.
A man may not forever chide or grieve.
So, learn to suffer, or I swear you've got
To learn the hard way, if you like it or not.

Some say that love's a little boy,
    And some say it's a bird,
Some say it makes the world go round,
    And some say that's absurd,
And when I asked the man next-door,
    Who looked as if he knew,
His wife got very cross indeed,
    And said it wouldn't do.

    Does it look like a pair of pyjamas,
      Or the ham in a temperance hotel?
    Does its odour remind one of llamas,
      Or has it a comforting smell?
    Is it prickly to touch as a hedge is,
      Or soft as eiderdown fluff?
    Is it sharp or quite smooth at the edges?
      O tell me the truth about love.

Our history books refer to it
    In cryptic little notes,
It's quite a common topic on
    The Transatlantic boats;
I've found the subject mentioned in
    Accounts of suicides,
And even seen it scribbled on
    The backs of railway-guides.

    Does it howl like a hungry Alsatian,
      Or boom like a military band?
    Could one give a first-rate imitation
      On a saw or a Steinway Grand?
    Is its singing at parties a riot?
      Does it only like Classical stuff?
    Will it stop when one wants to be quiet?
      O tell me the truth about love.

I looked inside the summer-house;
    It wasn't ever there:
I tried the Thames at Maidenhead,
    And Brighton's bracing air.
I don't know what the blackbird sang,
    Or what the tulip said;
But it wasn't in the chicken-run
    Or underneath the bed.

    Can it pull extraordinary faces?
        Is it usually sick on a swing?
    Does it spend all its time at the races,
        Or fiddling with pieces of string?
    Has it views of its own about money?
        Does it think Patriotism enough?
    Are its stories vulgar but funny?
        O tell me the truth about love.

    When it comes, will it come without warning,
        Just as I'm picking my nose?
    Will it knock on my door in the morning,
        Or tread in the bus on my toes?
    Will it come like a change in the weather?
        Will its greeting be courteous or rough?
    Will it alter my life altogether?
        O tell me the truth about love.

GEORGE PEELE

What Thing is Love?

What thing is love? For, well I wot, love is a thing.
It is a prick, it is a sting,
It is a pretty, pretty thing;
It is a fire, it is a coal,
Whose flame creeps in at every hole;
And as my wit doth best devise,
Love's dwelling is in ladies' eyes,
From whence do glance love's piercing darts,
That make such holes into our hearts;
And all the world herein accord,
Love is a great and mighty lord;
And when he list to mount so high,
With Venus he in heaven doth lie,
And evermore hath been a god,
Since Mars and she played even and odd.

RICHARD CRASHAW

from *Epithalamium*

XI

Long may this happy heaven-tied band
　　exercise its most holy art,
keeping her heart within his hand,
　　keeping his hand upon her heart,
　　　　but from her eyes
　　　　　　feel he no charms,
　　　　find she no joy
　　　　　　but in his arms;
May each maintain a well-fledged nest
of winged loves in either's breast,
Be each of them a mutual sacrifice
　　　　Of either's eyes:

XII

May their whole life a sweet song prove
　　set to two well-composed parts,
by music's noblest master, Love,
　　played on the strings of both their hearts;
　　　　whose mutual sound
　　　　　　may ever meet
　　　　in a just round,
　　　　　　not short though sweet;
Long may heaven listen to the song,
and think it short though it be long;
oh prove't a well-set song indeed, which shows
　　　　sweetest in the Close.

DANNIE ABSE

Epithalamion

Singing, today I married my white girl
beautiful in a barley field.
Green on thy finger a grass blade curled,
so with this ring I thee wed, I thee wed,
and send our love to the loveless world
of all the living and all the dead.

Now, no more than vulnerable human,
we, more than one, less than two,
are nearly ourselves in a barley field –
and only love is the rent that's due
though the bailiffs of time return anew
to all the living but not the dead.

Shipwrecked, the sun sinks down harbours
of a sky, unloads its liquid cargoes
of marigolds, and I and my white girl
lie still in the barley – who else wishes
to speak, what more can be said
by all the living against all the dead?

Come then all you wedding guests:
green ghost of trees, gold of barley,
you blackbird priests in the field,
you wind that shakes the pansy head
fluttering on a stalk like a butterfly;
come the living and come the dead.

Listen flowers, birds, winds, worlds,
tell all today that I married
more than a white girl in the barley –
for today I took to my human bed
flower and bird and wind and world,
and all the living and all the dead.

GERARD MANLEY HOPKINS

At the Wedding March

God with honour hang your head,
Groom, and grace you, bride, your bed
With lissome scions, sweet scions,
Out of hallowed bodies bred.

Each be other's comfort kind:
Déep, déeper than divined,
Divine charity, dear charity,
Fast you ever, fast bind.

Then let the March tread our ears:
I to him turn with tears
Who to wedlock, his wonder wedlock,
Déals tríumph and immortal years.

PHILIP LARKIN

The Whitsun Weddings

That Whitsun, I was late getting away:
   Not till about
One-twenty on the sunlit Saturday
Did my three-quarters-empty train pull out,
All windows down, all cushions hot, all sense
Of being in a hurry gone. We ran
Behind the backs of houses, crossed a street
Of blinding windscreens, smelt the fish-dock; thence
The river's level drifting breadth began,
Where sky and Lincolnshire and water meet.

All afternoon, through the tall heat that slept
   For miles inland,
A slow and stopping curve southwards we kept.
Wide farms went by, short-shadowed cattle, and
Canals with floatings of industrial froth;
A hothouse flashed uniquely: hedges dipped
And rose: and now and then a smell of grass
Displaced the reek of buttoned carriage-cloth
Until the next town, new and nondescript,
Approached with acres of dismantled cars.

At first, I didn't notice what a noise
   The weddings made
Each station that we stopped at: sun destroys
The interest of what's happening in the shade,
And down the long cool platforms whoops and skirls
I took for porters larking with the mails,
And went on reading. Once we started, though,
We passed them, grinning and pomaded, girls
In parodies of fashion, heels and veils,
All posed irresolutely, watching us go,

As if out on the end of an event
　　Waving goodbye
To something that survived it. Struck, I leant
More promptly out next time, more curiously,
And saw it all again in different terms:
The fathers with broad belts under their suits
And seamy foreheads; mothers loud and fat;
An uncle shouting smut; and then the perms,
The nylon gloves and jewellery-substitutes,
The lemons, mauves, and olive-ochres that

Marked off the girls unreally from the rest.
　　Yes, from cafés
And banquet-halls up yards, and bunting-dressed
Coach-party annexes, the wedding-days
Were coming to an end. All down the line
Fresh couples climbed aboard: the rest stood round;
The last confetti and advice were thrown,
And, as we moved, each face seemed to define
Just what it saw departing: children frowned
At something dull; fathers had never known

Success so huge and wholly farcical;
　　The women shared
The secret like a happy funeral;
While girls, gripping their handbags tighter, stared
At a religious wounding. Free at last,
And loaded with the sum of all they saw,
We hurried towards London, shuffling gouts of steam.
Now fields were building-plots, and poplars cast
Long shadows over major roads, and for
Some fifty minutes, that in time would seem

Just long enough to settle hats and say
  I nearly died,
A dozen marriages got under way.
They watched the landscape, sitting side by side
– An Odeon went past, a cooling tower,
And someone running up to bowl – and none
Thought of the others they would never meet
Or how their lives would all contain this hour.
I thought of London spread out in the sun,
Its postal districts packed like squares of wheat:

There we were aimed. And as we raced across
  Bright knots of rail
Past standing Pullmans, walls of blackened moss
Came close, and it was nearly done, this frail
Travelling coincidence; and what it held
Stood ready to be loosed with all the power
That being changed can give. We slowed again,
And as the tightened brakes took hold, there swelled
A sense of falling, like an arrow-shower
Sent out of sight, somewhere becoming rain.

BRIAN PATTEN

Yes

Last night I dreamt again of Adam returning
To the Garden's scented, bubbling cauldron.

Eve was beside him,
Their shadows were cut adrift
And the hum of bees was in their blood,

And the world was slow and good and all
The warm and yearning newness of their flesh
Was fixed forever in the glow of 'Yes'.

Continuations

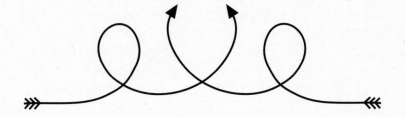

PHILIP LARKIN

Wedding-Wind

The wind blew all my wedding-day,
And my wedding-night was the night of the high wind;
And a stable door was banging, again and again,
That he must go and shut it, leaving me
Stupid in candlelight, hearing rain,
Seeing my face in the twisted candlestick,
Yet seeing nothing. When he came back
He said the horses were restless, and I was sad
That any man or beast that night should lack
The happiness I had.

               Now in the day
All's ravelled under the sun by the wind's blowing.
He has gone to look at the floods, and I
Carry a chipped pail to the chicken-run,
Set it down, and stare. All is the wind
Hunting through clouds and forests, thrashing
My apron and the hanging cloths on the line.
Can it be borne, this bodying-forth by wind
Of joy my actions turn on, like a thread
Carrying beads? Shall I be let to sleep
Now this perpetual morning shares my bed?
Can even death dry up
These new delighted lakes, conclude
Our kneeling as cattle by all-generous waters?

HELEN FOLEY

Touch Wood

Touch wood, be humble, never dare to say
That this is joy lest satisfaction throw
A shade on love which now (while roots still grow)
Stands like the proudest chestnut tree in May
With all its candles burning. Passions sway:
This has no tide nor any ebb and flow;
It has no evening, no red afterglow,
And needs no moon to keep the night at bay.

But since most lovers falter or contend,
And all their promises and all their powers
Drift towards a common grave, what chance have we?
Poets keep the past and priests eternity;
Only the day, the flying day is ours,
But while we hold it fast it cannot end.

MICHAEL BLUMENTHAL

A Marriage

You are holding up a ceiling
with both arms. It is very heavy,
but you must hold it up, or else
it will fall down on you. Your arms
are tired, terribly tired,
and, as the day goes on, it feels
as if either your arms or the ceiling
will soon collapse.

But then,
unexpectedly,
something wonderful happens:
Someone,
a man or a woman,
walks into the room
and holds their arms up
to the ceiling beside you.

So you finally get
to take down your arms.
You feel the relief of respite,
the blood flowing back
to your fingers and arms.
And when your partner's arms tire,
you hold up your own
to relieve him again.

And it can go on like this
for many years
without the house falling.

MARGARET ATWOOD

Habitation

Marriage is not
a house or even a tent

it is before that, and colder:

the edge of the forest, the edge
of the desert
            the unpainted stairs
at the back where we squat
outside, eating popcorn

the edge of the receding glacier

where painfully and with wonder
at having survived even
this far

we are learning to make fire

OGDEN NASH

A Word to Husbands

To keep your marriage brimming,
With love in the loving cup,
Whenever you're wrong, admit it;
Whenever you're right, shut up.

THOMAS MOORE

Oh, no – not even when first we loved
   Wert thou as dear as now thou art;
Thy beauty then my senses moved,
   But now thy virtues bind my heart.
What was but passion's sigh before,
   Has since been turned to reason's vow;
And, though I then might love thee more
   Trust me, I love thee better now.

Although my heart in earlier youth
   Might kindle with more wild desire,
Believe me, it has gained in truth
   Much more than it has lost in fire.
The flame now warms my inmost core,
   That then but sparkled over my brow,
And, though I seemed to love thee more,
   Yet, oh, I love thee better now.

The Anniversary

All kings, and all their favourites,
　All glory of honours, beauties, wits,
The sun itself, which makes times, as they pass,
Is elder by a year, now, than it was
When thou and I first one another saw:
All other things to their destruction draw,
　Only our love hath no decay;
This, no tomorrow hath, nor yesterday,
Running it never runs from us away,
But truly keeps his first, last, everlasting day.

Two graves must hide thine and my corse;
　If one might, death were no divorce.
Alas, as well as other princes, we
(Who prince enough in one another be)
Must leave at last in death, these eyes and ears,
Oft fed with true oaths, and with sweet salt tears;
　But souls where nothing dwells but love
(All other thoughts being inmates) then shall prove
This, or a love increased there above,
When bodies to their graves, souls from their
　　graves remove.

And then we shall be throughly blessed;
　But we no more than all the rest.
Here upon earth we are kings, and none but we
Can be such kings, nor of such subjects be;
Who is so safe as we? where none can do
Treason to us, except one of us two.
　True and false fears let us refrain,
Let us love nobly, and live, and add again
Years and years unto years, till we attain
To write threescore: this is the second of our reign.

MAURICE RIORDAN

The Table

Remember that table we used to want?
That we agreed should be plain, serviceable wood,
with drop leaves, to complete our tiny room.

Something to which baby-chairs could be yoked,
that might expand, in time, for supper-parties,
for renewed experiments with the spirit lamp.

Across which, over the wine and profiteroles,
we could tell each other stories: how I was thrown
off a buckrake under the back wheel of the tractor;

while you, a girl in Ontario, stuck your barrette
in a socket and were saved from electrocution
by its rubber band. You'd gloss *barrette* as hair-slide.

And we'd agree these were simultaneous events,
so we might chuckle once more at the providence
of coming together, to increase and multiply,

here, around a table we'd hunted down in New Cross,
having perambulated your bump (the twin-tub!)
through loft upon loft of displaced furniture.

We never gave up on that table, you know,
not officially. And I've kept an eye out for it,
scanning from habit the small ads and auction lists.

Would you believe me now if I telephoned
to say I'd found one? Nothing fancy or antique,
but an honest specimen of forties joinery.

It would require work. That marbled green veneer
would have to go, along with several nicks
and gouges, obscure stains, other people's memories.

Sure – a lot of work. But you can still see
somewhere inside it the original shining deal,
the plain altar still fit for household ceremonies.

SHARON OLDS

Primitive

I have heard about the civilized,
the marriages run on talk, elegant and
honest, rational. But you and I
are savages. You come in with a bag,
hold it out to me in silence.
I know Moo Shu Pork when I smell it
and understand the message: I have
pleased you greatly last night. We sit
quietly, side by side, to eat,
the long pancakes dangling and spilling,
fragrant sauce dripping out,
and glance at each other askance, wordless,
the corners of our eyes clear as spear points
laid along the sill to show
a friend sits with a friend here.

A. A. MILNE

Us Two

Wherever I am, there's always Pooh,
There's always Pooh and Me.
Whatever I do, he wants to do,
'Where are you going today?' says Pooh:
'Well, that's very odd 'cos I was too.
Let's go together,' says Pooh, says he.
'Let's go together,' says Pooh.

'What's twice eleven?' I said to Pooh.
('Twice what?' said Pooh to Me.)
'I *think* it ought to be twenty-two.'
'Just what I think myself,' said Pooh.
'It wasn't an easy sum to do,
But that's what it is,' said Pooh, said he.
'That's what it is,' said Pooh.

'Let's look for dragons,' I said to Pooh.
'Yes, let's,' said Pooh to Me.
We crossed the river and found a few –
'Yes, those are dragons all right,' said Pooh.
'As soon as I saw their beaks I knew.
That's what they are,' said Pooh, said he.
'That's what they are,' said Pooh.

'Let's frighten the dragons,' I said to Pooh.
'That's right,' said Pooh to Me.
'*I'm* not afraid,' I said to Pooh,
And I held his paw and I shouted 'Shoo!
Silly old dragons!' – and off they flew.

'I wasn't afraid,' said Pooh, said he,
'I'm *never* afraid with you.'

So wherever I am, there's always Pooh,
There's always Pooh and Me.
'What would I do?' I said to Pooh,
'If it wasn't for you,' and Pooh said: 'True,
It isn't much fun for One, but Two
Can stick together,' says Pooh, says he.
'That's how it is,' says Pooh.

AMY LOWELL

A Decade

When you came, you were like red wine and honey,
And the taste of you burnt my mouth with its sweetness.
Now you are like morning bread,
Smooth and pleasant.
I hardly taste you at all for I know your savour,
But I am completely nourished.

EMILY BRONTË

Love and Friendship

Love is like the wild rose-briar,
Friendship like the holly-tree –
The holly is dark when the rose-briar blooms
But which will bloom most constantly?

The wild rose-briar is sweet in spring,
Its summer blossoms scent the air;
Yet wait till winter comes again
And who will call the wild-briar fair?

Then scorn the silly rose-wreath now
And deck thee with the holly's sheen,
That when December blights thy brow
He still may leave thy garland green.

D. H. LAWRENCE

Fidelity

Fidelity and love are two different things, like a flower
    and a gem.
And love, like a flower, will fade, will change into something
    else
or it would not be flowery.

O flowers they fade because they are moving swiftly; a little
    torrent of life
leaps up to the summit of the stem, gleams, turns over round
    the bend
of the parabola of curved flight,
sinks, and is gone, like a comet curving into the invisible.

O flowers, they are all the time travelling
like comets, and they come into our ken
for a day, for two days, and withdraw, slowly vanish again.

And we, we must take them on the wing, and let them go.
Embalmed flowers are not flowers, immortelles are not flowers;
flowers are just a motion, a swift motion, a coloured gesture;
that is their loveliness. And that is love.

But a gem is different. It lasts so much longer than we do
so much much much much longer
that it seems to last for ever.
Yet we know it is flowing away
as flowers are, and we are, only slower.
The wonderful slow flowing of the sapphire!

All flows, and every flow is related to every other flow.
Flowers and sapphires and us, diversely streaming.

In the old days, when sapphires were breathed upon and
    brought forth
during the wild orgasms of chaos
time was much slower, when the rocks came forth.
It took aeons to make a sapphire, aeons for it to pass away.

And a flower it takes a summer.

And man and woman are like the earth, that brings forth flowers
in summer, and love, but underneath is rock.
Older than flowers, older than ferns, older than foraminiferæ,
older than plasm altogether is the soul of a man underneath.

And when, throughout all the wild orgasms of love
slowly a gem forms, in the ancient, once-more-molten rocks
of two human hearts, two ancient rocks, a man's heart and a
    woman's,
that is the crystal of peace, the slow hard jewel of trust,
the sapphire of fidelity.
The gem of mutual peace emerging from the wild chaos of love.

THOMAS CAMPBELL

Song

How delicious is the winning
Of a kiss at Love's beginning,
When two mutual hearts are sighing
For the knot there's no untying!

Yet remember, 'midst our wooing,
Love has bliss, but Love has ruing;
Other smiles may make you fickle,
Tears for other charms may trickle.

Love he comes, and Love he tarries,
Just as fate or fancy carries;
Longest stays when sorest chidden,
Laughs and flies when pressed and bidden.

Bind the sea to slumber stilly,
Bind its odour to the lily,
Bind the aspen ne'er to quiver,
Then bind Love to last for ever!

Love's a fire that needs renewal
Of fresh beauty for its fuel:
Love's wing moults when caged and captured,
Only free he soars enraptured.

Can you keep the bee from ranging,
Or the ringdove's neck from changing?
No! nor fettered Love from dying
In the knot there's no untying.

SAMUEL BISHOP

To His Wife
on the Fourteenth Anniversary
of Her Wedding-Day, With a Ring

'Thee, Mary, with this ring I wed,'
So, fourteen years ago, I said.
Behold another ring! 'For what?'
'To wed thee over again – why not?

With that first ring I married youth,
Grace, beauty, innocence, and truth;
Taste long admired, sense long revered,
And all my Molly then appeared.

If she, by merit since disclosed,
Prove twice the woman I supposed,
I plead that double merit now,
To justify a double vow.

Here, then, today, with faith as sure,
With ardour as intense, as pure,
As when, amidst the rite divine,
I took thy troth, and plighted mine,

To thee, sweet girl, my second ring
A token and a pledge I bring:
With this I wed, till death us part,
Thy riper virtues to my heart;
Those virtues which, before untried,
The wife has added to the bride;
Those virtues, whose progressive claim,
Endearing wedlock's very name,
My soul enjoys, my song approves,
For conscience' sake as well as love's.

For why? They show me every hour
Honour's high thought, affection's power,
Discretion's deed, sound judgement's sentence,
And teach me all things – but repentance.'

To — —

I

When passion's trance is overpast,
If tenderness and truth could last,
Or live, whilst all wild feelings keep
Some mortal slumber, dark and deep,
I should not weep, I should not weep!

II

It were enough to feel, to see,
Thy soft eyes gazing tenderly,
And dream the rest – and burn and be
The secret food of fires unseen,
Could thou but be as thou hast been.

III

After the slumber of the year
The woodland violets reappear;
All things revive in field or grove,
And sky and sea, but two, which move
And form all others, life and love.

I

So, we'll go no more a roving
  So late into the night,
Though the heart be still as loving,
  And the moon be still as bright.

II

For the sword outwears its sheath,
  And the soul wears out the breast,
And the heart must pause to breathe,
  And love itself have rest.

III

Though the night was made for loving,
  And the day returns too soon,
Yet we'll go no more a roving
  By the light of the moon.

W. B. YEATS

When You are Old

When you are old and grey and full of sleep,
And nodding by the fire, take down this book,
And slowly read, and dream of the soft look
Your eyes had once, and of their shadows deep;

How many loved your moments of glad grace,
And loved your beauty with love false or true,
But one man loved the pilgrim soul in you,
And loved the sorrows of your changing face;

And bending down beside the glowing bars,
Murmur, a little sadly, how Love fled
And paced upon the mountains overhead
And hid his face amid a crowd of stars.

EDITH WHARTON

from *The Mortal Lease*

VIII

Strive we no more. Some hearts are like the bright
Tree-chequered spaces, flecked with sun and shade,
Where gathered in old days the youth and maid
To woo, and weave their dances; with the night
They cease their flutings, and the next day's light
Finds the smooth green unconscious of their tread,
And ready its velvet pliancies to spread
Under fresh feet, till these in turn take flight.

But other hearts a long long road doth span,
From some far region of old works and wars,
And the weary armies of the thoughts of man
Have trampled it, and furrowed it with scars,
And sometimes, husht, a sacred caravan
Moves over it alone, beneath the stars.

GLYN MAXWELL

Stargazing

The night is fine and dry. It falls and spreads
the cold sky with a million opposites
that, for a moment, seem like a million souls
and soon, none, and then, for what seems a long time,
one. Then of course it spins. What is better to do
than string out over the infinite dead spaces
the ancient beasts and spearmen of the human
mind, and, if not the real ones, new ones?

But, try making them clear to one you love –
whoever is standing by you is one you love
when pinioned by the stars – you will find it quite
impossible, but like her more for thinking
she sees that constellation.

After the wave of pain, you will turn to her
and, in an instant, change the universe
to a sky you were glad you came outside to see.

This is the act of all the descended gods
of every age and creed: to weary of all
that never ends, to take a human hand,
and go back into the house.

R. S. THOMAS

Luminary

My luminary,
my morning and evening
star. My light at noon
when there is no sun
and the sky lowers. My balance
of joy in a world
that has gone off joy's
standard. Yours the face
that young I recognised
as though I had known you
of old. Come, my eyes
said, out into the morning
of a world whose dew
waits for your footprint.
Before a green altar
with the thrush for priest
I took those gossamer
vows that neither the Church
could stale nor the Machine
tarnish, that with the years
have grown hard as flint,
lighter than platinum
on our ringless fingers.

Looking Back in My Eighty-First Year

How did we get to be old ladies –
my grandmother's job – when we
were the long-leggèd girls?

–Hilma Wolitzer

Instead of marrying the day after graduation,
in spite of freezing on my father's arm as
here comes the bride struck up,
saying, I'm not sure I want to do this,

I should have taken that fellowship
to the University of Grenoble to examine
the original manuscript
of Stendhal's unfinished *Lucien Leuwen*,

I, who had never been west of the Mississippi,
should have crossed the ocean
in third class on the Cunard White Star,
the war just over, the Second World War

when Kilroy was here, that innocent graffito,
two eyes and a nose draped over
a fence line. How could I go?
Passion had locked us together.

Sixty years my lover,
he says he would have waited.
He says he would have sat
where the steamship docked

till the last of the pursers
decamped, and I rushed back
littering the runway with carbon paper . . .
Why didn't I go? It was fated.

Marriage dizzied us. Hand over hand,
flesh against flesh for the final haul,
we tugged our lifeline through limestone and sand,
lover and long-leggèd girl.

EDWIN MUIR

The Commemoration

I wish I could proclaim
My faith enshrined in you
And spread among a few
Our high but hidden fame,
That we new life have spun
Past all that's thought and done,
And someone or no one
Might tell both did the same.

Material things will pass
And we have seen the flower
And the slow falling tower
Lie gently in the grass,
But meantime we have stored
Riches past bed and board
And nursed another hoard
Than callow lad and lass.

Invisible virtue now
Expands upon the air
Although no fruit appear
Nor weight bend down the bough,
And harvests truly grown
For someone or no one
Are stored and safely won
In hollow heart and brow.

How can one thing remain
Except the invisible,
The echo of a bell
Long rusted in the rain?
This strand we weave into
Our monologue of two,
And time cannot undo
That strong and subtle chain.

FRANK O'HARA

Animals

Have you forgotten what we were like then
when we were still first rate
and the day came fat with an apple in its mouth

it's no use worrying about Time
but we did have a few tricks up our sleeves
and turned some sharp corners

the whole pasture looked like our meal
we didn't need speedometers
we could manage cocktails out of ice and water

I wouldn't want to be faster
or greener than now if you were with me O you
were the best of all my days

HUGO WILLIAMS

The Time of Our Lives

The future can go and be
bloody terrifying on its own
for all I care. Me and my girl
are stepping out for the past.
We're putting our best foot
backwards, heading for home.
What we'll do when we get there
we haven't decided yet.
For the time being at least
we're having the time of our lives
all over again.

LOUIS MACNEICE

All Over Again

As if I had known you for years drink to me only if
Those frontiers had never changed on the mad map of the years
And all our tears were earned and this were the first cliff
From which we embraced the sea and these were the first words
We spread to lure the birds that nested in our day
As if it were always morning their dawnsong theirs and ours
And waking no one else me and you only now
Under the brow of a blue and imperturbable hill
Where still time stands and plays his bland and hemlock pipe
And the ripe moment tugs yet declines to fall and all
The years we had not met forget themselves in this
One kiss ingathered world and outward rippling bell
To the rim of the cup of the sky and leave it only there
Near into far blue into blue all over again
Notwithstanding unique all over all again
Of which to speak requires new fires of the tongue some trick
Of the light in the dark of the muted voice of the turning wild
World yet calm in her storm gay in her ancient rocks
To preserve today one kiss in this skybound timeless cup
Nor now shall I ask for anything more of future or past
This being last and first sound sight on eyes and ears
And each long then and there suspended on this cliff
Shining and slicing edge that reflects the sun as if
This one Between were All and we in love for years.

CAROL ANN DUFFY

Finding the Words

I found the words at the back of a drawer,
wrapped in black cloth, like three rings
slipped from a dead woman's hand, cold,
dull gold. I had held them before,

                         years ago,
then put them away, forgetting whatever it was
I could use them to say. I touched the first to my lips,
the second, the third, like a sacrament,
like a pledge, like a kiss,

               and my breath
warmed them, the words I needed to utter this, small words,
and few. I rubbed at them till they gleamed in my palm –
I love you, I love you, I love you –
as though they were new.

GEORGE CRABBE

A Wedding Ring

The ring so worn, as you behold,
So thin, so pale, is yet of gold:
The passion such it was to prove;
Worn with life's cares, love yet was love.

Confetti

Permit me voyage, love, into your hands . . .

Hart Crane

MIRANDA: I am your wife, if you will marry me [. . .]
  My husband then?
FERDINAND: Ay, with a heart as willing
  As bondage e'er of freedom. Here's my hand.

William Shakespeare

And the sunlight clasps the earth,
  And the moonbeams kiss the sea:
What is all this sweet work worth
  If thou kiss not me?

Percy Bysshe Shelley

'Love me, for I love you' – and answer me,
'Love me, for I love you' – so we shall stand
As happy equals in the flowering land
Of love, that knows not a dividing sea.

Christina Rossetti

I ascend, I float in the regions of your love O man,
O sharer of my roving life.

Walt Whitman

Write me my new future's epigraph,
New angel mine, unhoped for in the world!

Elizabeth Barrett Browning

I would I could adopt your will,
See with your eyes, and set my heart
Beating by yours, and drink my fill
At your soul's springs, – your part my part
In life, for good and ill.

Robert Browning

Drink to me only with thine eyes,
    And I will pledge with mine;
Or leave a kiss in the cup,
    And I'll not look for wine.

Ben Jonson

If I have freedom in my Love,
    And in my soul am free;
Angels alone that soar above,
    Enjoy such liberty.

Richard Lovelace

To love you without stint and all I can
Today, tomorrow, world without an end.

Christina Rossetti

How blest I am in this discovering thee!
To enter into these bonds, is to be free;
Then where my hand is set, my seal shall be.

John Donne

Why do I love? Go, ask the glorious sun
Why every day it round the world doth run.

'Ephelia'

Thou, O my soul, my flesh, and my blood!
Then come the wild weather, come sleet or come snow,
We will stand by each other, however it blow.

Henry Wadsworth Longfellow

So are you to my thoughts as food to life
Or as sweet-seasoned showers are to the ground.

William Shakespeare

You, that are the sovereign of my heart,
Have all my joys attending on your will.

Charles Best

Oh! those were golden hours,
When Love, devoid of cares,
In all Arcadia's bowers
Lodged swains and nymphs by pairs!

John Gay

Mankind should hope, in wedlock's state,
A friend to find as well as mate.

Mary Savage

What is it men in women do require?
The lineaments of Gratified Desire.
What is it women do in men require?
The lineaments of Gratified Desire.

William Blake

Happy be the bridegroom,
And happy be the bride;
And may not man, nor bird, nor beast
This happy pair divide.

Anonymous

Again the feast, the speech, the glee,
The shade of passing thought, the wealth
Of words and wit, the double health,
The crowning cup, the three-times-three.

Alfred, Lord Tennyson

The bloated wassaillers will never heed –
Let us away, my love, with happy speed.

John Keats

Joy to the bridegroom and the bride
That lie by one another's side!

Thomas Randolph

When a man has married a wife, he finds out whether
Her knees and elbows are only glued together.

William Blake

Yet still I love thee without art,
Ancient person of my heart.

John Wilmot, Earl of Rochester

True love is a durable fire,
In the mind ever burning,
Never sick, never old, never dead,
From itself never turning.

Sir Walter Ralegh

Love that first its glory gave
Shall be my pole star to the grave.

Emily Brontë

Acknowledgements

For kindly sharing with me their favourite poems, and in many cases for their practical help or wise advice, I owe my thanks to Helen Adie, Ellah Allfrey, Ronald Asprey, Tim Atkin, Diane Bourke, Suzanne Brandreth, Samuel Brookes, Chloe Campbell, Charles Cumming, Sasha Dugdale, Joe Dunthorne, Ben Faccini, Maggie Fergusson, Hélène Fiamma, William Fiennes, Jamie Glazebrook, Catherine Hall, Sally Harding, Sara Holloway, Cynan Jones, Philip Gwyn Jones, Kapka Kassabova, Mark Kessler, Hilary Laurie, Anne Marsella, Hannah Marshall, Olivia McCannon, Anne Meadows, James Meek, Richard Meier, Juliette Mitchell, Matthew Parker, Max Porter, Simon Prosser, Kamila Shamsie, Anna South, Anna Stein, Lorin Stein, Joy Tadaki, Adam Thirlwell, Martin Toseland, Simon Trewin, and Saradha Soobrayen and the staff at the Saison Poetry Library, and the staff at the London Library. For the 'ever-fixèd mark' of their friendship, I am most especially grateful to Claire Allfree, Stephen Brown, Nina Caplan and Victoria Moore.

And at Penguin, thanks to Simon Winder, Anna Hervé, Ian Pindar, Kristina Blagojevitch and Coralie Bickford-Smith.

I dedicate this volume to Susan and John Barber, and Florence and Ian Knapp, with love.

The editors and publisher gratefully acknowledge the following for permission to reprint copyright material:

DANNIE ABSE: 'Epithalamion' from New and Collected Poems (Hutchinson, 2003), copyright © Dannie Abse, 2003. Reprinted by permission of United Agents on behalf of Dr Dannie Abse.

JOHN AGARD: 'Nuptials' from Travel Light, Travel Dark (Bloodaxe, 2013), copyright © John Agard, 2013. Reprinted by permission of Bloodaxe Books.

MARGARET ATWOOD: 'Habitation' from Procedures for Underground, in Poems: 1965–1975 (Houghton Mifflin, 1976; OUP Canada, 1976; Virago Press, 1991). Copyright © Margaret Atwood, 1976. Reprinted by permission of Curtis Brown Group Ltd, on behalf of Margaret Atwood.

W. H. AUDEN: 'Twelve Songs: XII [Some say that love's a little boy]', copyright © 1940 and renewed 1968 by W. H. Auden; and 'Ten Songs: IV [Carry her over the water]', copyright © 1941 by Hawkes & Son (London) Ltd, and copyright 1945 by W. H. Auden. Copyright renewed 1973 by The Estate of W. H. Auden W. H. Auden Collected Poems by W. H. Auden. Reprinted by

SOPHIE HANNAH: 'Match' from A Woman's Life and Loves, in *First of the Last Chances* (Carcanet, 2003), copyright © Sophie Hannah, 2003. Reprinted by permission of Carcanet Press Ltd.

SEAMUS HEANEY: 'Scaffolding' from *Death of a Naturalist* (Faber and Faber, 1966), copyright © Seamus Heaney, 1966. Reprinted by permission of Faber and Faber.

ADRIAN HENRI: 'Love is. . . ' from *Collected Poems* (Allison & Busby Ltd, 1986), copyright © Adrian Henri, 1986. Reproduced by permission of the estate of Adrian Henri c/o Rogers, Coleridge & White, 20 Powis Mews, London, W11 1JN.

JANE HOLLAND: 'They Are a Tableau at the Kissing-Gate' from *The Brief History of a Disreputable Woman* (Bloodaxe, 1997), copyright © Jane Holland, 1997.

LANGSTON HUGHES: 'Harlem Night Song' from *The Weary Blues* (New York: Knopf, 1926) and *Selected Poems of Langston Hughes* (New York: Knopf, 1959), in *The Collected Poems of Langston Hughes* (New York: Knopf, 1994), copyright © 1994 the Estate of Langston Hughes. Reprinted by permission of David Higham Associates Ltd.

ELIZABETH JENNINGS: 'Love Poem' from *Relationships* (1972) in *The Collected Poems*, ed. Emma Mason (Carcanet, 2012), copyright © 2012 the Estate of Elizabeth Jennings. Reprinted by permission of David Higham Associates Ltd.

MIMI KHALVATI: 'Ghazal', copyright © Mimi Khalvati, 2006. Reprinted by permission of Carcanet Press Ltd on behalf of the author.

MAXINE KUMIN: 'Looking Back in My Eighty-First Year' from *Still to Mow*, in *Where I Love: New and Selected Poems 1990–2010* (W. W. Norton & Company, 2010). Reprinted by permission of W. W. Norton & Company.

NICK LAIRD: 'Estimates' from *To A Fault* (Faber and Faber, 2005), copyright © Nick Laird, 2005. Reprinted by permission of Faber and Faber.

PHILIP LARKIN: 'Is it for now or for always', 'The Whitsun Weddings' and 'Wedding-Wind' from *Collected Poems* (Faber and Faber, 2003), reprinted by permission of Faber and Faber.

LIZ LOCHHEAD: 'Epithalamium' from *The Colour of Black and White: Poems 1984–2003* (Polygon, 2003), copyright © Liz Lochhead, 2003. Reprinted by permission of Birlinn Ltd.

NORMAN MacCAIG: 'Sure proof' from *A Man in My Position* (1969), in *Collected Poems* (Chatto & Windus, 1990). Reprinted by permission of Birlinn Ltd on behalf of the Estate of Norman MacCaig.

ANNE MacLEOD: 'There will be no end' from *Standing by Thistles* (Scottish Cultural Press, 1997), copyright © Anne MacLeod, 1997. Reprinted by permission of the author.

LOUIS MacNEICE: 'All Over Again' from *Collected Poems*, ed. E. R. Dodds (Faber and Faber, 2007). Copyright © the Estate of Louis MacNeice. Reprinted by permission of David Higham Associates Ltd.

GLYN MAXWELL: 'Stargazing' from *Rest for the Wicked* (Bloodaxe, 1995), copyright © Glyn Maxwell, 1995. Reprinted by permission of Bloodaxe Books.

JAMES MCAULEY: 'One Thing At Least' from *Surprises of the Sun* in *Collected Poems 1936–1970* (Angus and Robertson, 1971), copyright © 1971 James McAuley. By arrangement with the Licensor, The James McAuley Estate, c/o Curtis Brown (Aust) Pty Ltd.

ROGER MCGOUGH: 'Vow' from *As Far As I Know* (Viking, 2012), copyright © Roger McGough, 2011. Reprinted by permission of United Agents on behalf of Roger McGough.

PETER MEINKE: 'The First Marriage' from *Scars* (University of Pittsburgh Press, 1996), copyright © 1996 Peter Meinke. Reprinted by permission of the University of Pittsburgh Press.

RICHARD MEIER: 'Moment' from *Misadventure* (Picador, 2012), reprinted by permission of the author, c/o Rogers, Coleridge & White, Ltd, 20 Powis Mews, London, W11 1JN.

WILLIAM MEREDITH: 'Tree Marriage' from *Efforts at Speech: New and Selected Poems* (TriQuarterly Books/ Northwestern University, 1997). Copyright © 1997 William Meredith. Reprinted by permission of Northwestern University Press and Richard Harteis.

A. A. MILNE: 'Us Two' from *Now We Are Six*, copyright © The Trustees of the Pooh Properties, 1927. Published by Egmont Books Limited, London, and used with permission.

EDWIN MUIR: 'The Confirmation' and 'The Commemoration' from *Collected Poems* (Faber and Faber, 2003), copyright © Willa Muir, 1960. Reprinted by permission of Faber and Faber.

OGDEN NASH: 'A Word to Husbands' from *Everyone But Thee and Me* (1962) from *Candy is Dandy: The Best of Ogden Nash*, selected by Linell Smith and Isabel Eberstadt, with an introduction by Anthony Burgess (André Deutsch, 1994). Reproduced by permission of the Carlton Publishing Group and Curtis Brown Ltd.

FRANK O'HARA: 'Poem' and 'Animals' from *The Collected Poems of Frank O'Hara*, ed. Donald Allen, copyright © 1971 by Maureen Granville-Smith, Administratrix of the Estate of Frank O'Hara. Reprinted by permission of Alfred A. Knopf, a division of Random House, Inc., and Carcanet Press Ltd.

SHARON OLDS: 'Primitive' from *Satan Says* (1980) in *The Sign of Saturn: Poems 1980–1987* (Martin Secker & Warburg, 1991), copyright © Sharon Olds, 1980, 1991. Reprinted by permission of The Random House Group Ltd.

ALICE OSWALD: 'Wedding' from *The Thing in the Gap-Stone Stile* (Faber and Faber, 2007), copyright © Alice Oswald, 2007. Reprinted by permission of Faber and Faber.

DON PATERSON: 'The Trans-Siberian Express' from *Nil, Nil* (1993) in *Selected Poems* (Faber and Faber, 2012), copyright © Don Paterson, 2012. Reprinted by permission of Faber and Faber and the author, c/o Rogers, Coleridge & White, Ltd, 20 Powis Mews, London, W11 1JN.

BRIAN PATTEN: 'Her Song' and 'Yes' from *Love Poems* (Allen & Unwin,

Index of Poets

Index of Titles and First Lines